GRANTSMANSHIP

SAGE HUMAN SERVICES GUIDES, VOLUME 1
Second Edition

P9-DFP-451

SAGE HUMAN SERVICES GUIDES

A series of books edited by ARMAND LAUFFER and CHARLES D. GARVIN. Published in cooperation with the University of Michigan School of Social Work and other organizations.

1: **GRANTSMANSHIP** by Armand Lauffer (second edition)
5: **VOLUNTEERS** by Armand Lauffer and Sarah Gorodezky with Jay Callahan and Carla Overberger
10: **GROUP PARTICIPATION** by Harvey J. Bertcher
11: **BE ASSERTIVE** by Sandra Stone Sundel and Martin Sundel
14: **NEEDS ASSESSMENT** by Keith A. Neuber with William T. Atkins, James A. Jacobson, and Nicholas A. Reuterman
15: **DEVELOPING CASEWORK SKILLS** by James A. Pippin
17: **EFFECTIVE MEETINGS** by John E. Tropman
20: **CHANGING ORGANIZATIONS AND COMMUNITY PROGRAMS** by Jack Rothman, John L. Erlich, and Joseph G. Teresa
24: **CHANGING THE SYSTEM** by Milan J. Dluhy
25: **HELPING WOMEN COPE WITH GRIEF** by Phyllis R. Silverman
29: **EVALUATING YOUR AGENCY'S PROGRAMS** by Michael J. Austin, Gary Cox, Naomi Gottlieb, J. David Hawkins, Jean M. Kruzich, and Ronald Rauch
30: **ASSESSMENT TOOLS** by Armand Lauffer
31: **UNDERSTANDING PROGRAM EVALUATION** by Leonard Rutman and George Mowbray
33: **FAMILY ASSESSMENT** by Adele M. Holman
35: **SUPERVISION** by Eileen Gambrill and Theodore J. Stein
36: **BUILDING SUPPORT NETWORKS FOR THE ELDERLY** by David E. Biegel, Barbara K. Shore, and Elizabeth Gordon
37: **STRESS MANAGEMENT FOR HUMAN SERVICES** by Richard E. Farmer, Lynn Hunt Monohan, and Reinhold W. Hekeler
38: **FAMILY CAREGIVERS AND DEPENDENT ELDERLY** by Dianne Springer and Timothy H. Brubaker
39: **DESIGNING AND IMPLEMENTING PROCEDURES FOR HEALTH AND HUMAN SERVICES** by Morris Schaefer
40: **GROUP THERAPY WITH ALCOHOLICS** by Baruch Levine and Virginia Gallogly
41: **DYNAMIC INTERVIEWING** by Frank F. Maple
42: **THERAPEUTIC PRINCIPLES IN PRACTICE** by Herbert S. Strean
43: **CAREERS, COLLEAGUES, AND CONFLICTS** by Armand Lauffer

44: **PURCHASE OF SERVICE CONTRACTING** by Peter M. Kettner and Lawrence L. Martin
45: **TREATING ANXIETY DISORDERS** by Bruce A. Thyer
46: **TREATING ALCOHOLISM** by Norman K. Denzin
47: **WORKING UNDER THE SAFETY NET** by Steve Burghardt and Michael Fabricant
48: **MANAGING HUMAN SERVICES PERSONNEL** by Peter J. Pecora and Michael J. Austin
49: **IMPLEMENTING CHANGE IN SERVICE PROGRAMS** by Morris Schaefer
50: **PLANNING FOR RESEARCH** by Raymond M. Berger and Michael A. Patchner
51: **IMPLEMENTING THE RESEARCH PLAN** by Raymond M. Berger and Michael A. Patchner
52: **MANAGING CONFLICT** by Herb Bisno
53: **STRATEGIES FOR HELPING VICTIMS OF ELDER MISTREATMENT** by Risa S. Breckman and Ronald D. Adelman
54: **COMPUTERIZING YOUR AGENCY'S INFORMATION SYSTEM** by Denise E. Bronson, Donald C. Pelz, and Eileen Trzcinski
55: **HOW PERSONAL GROWTH AND TASK GROUPS WORK** by Robert K. Conyne
56: **COMMUNICATION BASICS FOR HUMAN SERVICE PROFESSIONALS** by Elam Nunnally and Caryl Moy
57: **COMMUNICATION DISORDERS IN AGING** edited by Raymond H. Hull and Kathleen M. Griffin
58: **THE PRACTICE OF CASE MANAGEMENT** by David P. Moxley
59: **MEASUREMENT IN DIRECT PRACTICE** by Betty J. Blythe and Tony Tripodi
60: **BUILDING COALITIONS IN THE HUMAN SERVICES** by Milan J. Dluhy with the assistance of Sanford L. Kravitz
61: **PSYCHIATRIC MEDICATIONS** by Kenneth J. Bender
62: **PRACTICE WISDOM** by Donald F. Krill
63: **PROPOSAL WRITING** by Soraya M. Coley and Cynthia A. Scheinberg
64: **QUALITY ASSURANCE FOR LONG-TERM CARE PROVIDERS** by William Ammentorp, Kenneth D. Gossett, and Nancy Euchner Poe
65: **GROUP COUNSELING WITH JUVENILE DELINQUENTS** by Matthew L. Ferrara

A **SAGE** HUMAN SERVICES GUIDE **1**

GRANTSMANSHIP
Second Edition

Armand LAUFFER

Published in cooperation with the University of Michigan
School of Social Work

SAGE PUBLICATIONS
The International Professional Publishers
Newbury Park   London   New Delhi

Copyright © 1983 by Sage Publications, Inc.

All rights reserved. No part of this book may be reproduced or utilized in any form or by any means, electronic or mechanical, including photocopying, recording, or by any information storage and retrieval system, without permission in writing from the publisher.

For information address:

SAGE Publications, Inc.
2455 Teller Road
Newbury Park, California 91320

SAGE Publications Ltd.
6 Bonhill Street
London EC2A 4PU
United Kingdom

SAGE Publications India Pvt. Ltd.
M-32 Market
Greater Kailash I
New Delhi 110 048 India

Printed in the United States of America

Library of Congress Cataloging in Publication Data

Lauffer, Armand.
  Grantsmanship. (second edition)

  (Sage human services guide ; 1)
  "Published in cooperation with the University of
Michigan School of Social Work."
  1. Fund raising. 2. Proposal writing in the social
sciences. I. Title. II. Series.
HG177.L375   1983   361.7   83-17741
ISBN 0-8039-2022-9 (pbk.)

  93 94 10 9 8 7

CONTENTS

Introduction and Acknowledgments   7
1. **The Business of Grantseeking
   and Fund Raising**   9
2. **Assessing Your Program's Marketability**   13
3. **The Bucks Start Here:**
   Seeking Government Funds   39
4. **Building on a Strong Foundation:**
   Seeking Foundation Grants   57
5. **The Business of Business Is Business:**
   Seeking Private Sector Funds   75
6. **Civic Duty:** Seeking Support from
   the Voluntary Sector   89
7. **Getting Organized:** Eight Steps Toward
   Writing a Proposal   107
8. **Writing the Project Proposal:**
   A Blueprint for Action   133
9. **Drawing Up the Budget**   149
10. **What to Do If You Don't Get Funded:**
    And What to Do If You Do or
    While You're Waiting to Find Out   167

Appendix A: Getting the Terms Straight   177

Appendix B: Grantsmanship Information Resources   183

About the Author   191

INTRODUCTION
AND
ACKNOWLEDGMENTS

You will find this book relatively easy reading. Using it may not be all that easy; and that is what the book is intended for — use; use in developing the skill to succeed at fund raising and grantseeking.

It is built on the experiences of many people; successful fund raisers and grantseekers who have been willing to share their insights with us. Your success will be built on what you do with the book and how you use the exercises to develop both analytic and interactional skills. Together both sets of skills make a powerful combination.

Some of you may recognize in these pages vestiges of my earlier book on *Grantsmanship*, but more than 90 percent of this volume is new. The 1980s are not the same as the 1970s. We have learned much since then. We have come to understand that living in an affluent society is no guarantee that affluence will be shared equitably. And we have learned that resources must not only be secured, but carefully harnessed to do the most good. I have personally learned a great deal from the dozens of successful fund raisers interviewed for this book and whose experiences are reflected in its pages. The vignettes are all taken from practice, although most were heavily disguised in order to maintain confidentiality. I am sure you will agree that we owe a vote of thanks to all those who contribute them. For my part, I want to thank Ann Page who whipped out the final draft of this manuscript in one week. We all owe a thank you to Glen Swier whose research generated some of the materials and private sector funding reported in Chapter 5, and many of the information resources described throught the book.

Armand Lauffer
Ann Arbor, Michigan,
Summer 1983

Chapter 1

THE BUSINESS OF GRANTSEEKING
AND FUND RAISING

VIGNETTE 1: TAKING NOTHING FOR GRANTED

Nothing happened, absolutely nothing. We sent our grant application to the foundation, got a postcard saying it was of interest and that it would be reviewed within 3 months. When we got no further word at the end of six months, I wrote a letter inquiring as to the status of our proposal. It was a year before we finally got our reply. We were turned down. Luckily, we were no longer dependent on the foundation. By then we had decided to let the whole idea die a natural death.

That may not be the most encouraging way of being introduced to grantsmanship. Unfortunately, it is an experience shared by all too many of us who begin with good intentions, and perhaps with the conviction that what we are doing is important and deserving of support. That is not a bad way to begin. But it must be supported with skill and hard work. Will all the results be worth the effort? The answer can be an affirmative yes, even if you do not get funded. It depends on the way in which you phrase the next question.

If you ask, "What are our chances of getting the support we need to do our business?", the reply throughout the 1980s is likely to be "Not very good." Now let us try another question: "What are our chances of getting the support needed to do business?" The answer is "Not bad." In fact, it is probably pretty good, if you are clear about whose business you are doing.

Human service and other nonprofit organizations are in the business of doing the public's business. The support you are going to be able to muster will depend on the extent to which its various publics perceive the organization's activities as being in their interests. Successful fund raisers have always known that. Unlike the person quoted, they are not resigned to letting projects die a natural death. It is rarely sufficient to send a proposal off and then wait to see what the potential funding source does with it. When it comes to grants, if you will pardon the pun, "take nothing for granted." Prepare for both acceptance or rejection. Prepare the funding source to deal with your proposal or ideas and prepare other key publics.

In the narrow sense, this is a book about grantsmanship and related fund-raising activities. In a broader sense it is about program and resource development, and about articulating your organization's interests with those of suppliers, consumers, and other publics. Without them your organization would have no resources and no business.

GETTING THE RESOURCES YOU NEED

We tend to use the term "resources" to mean money. It does, but it is not limited to money. Resources are all those means and commodities needed to achieve an objective, produce a service, or distribute a product. Some resources, such as facilities, equipment, and supplies, are purchaseable with money or can be used in lieu of cash. Other resources, such as legitimacy, expertise, and commitment may or may not be related to money. They are, nevertheless, indispensable to the conduct of organizational affairs. Without them, program and resource development are hardly likely to be successful.

This will become clear as you progress through this guide. In the next chapter, for example, we will examine your program's marketability: its ability to attract resources, to transform those resources into products, and to attract consumers to programs and services. To a large extent that ability will be bolstered by your skill in using one resource to make do in substitution for another and to attract still others.

Chapters 3 through 6 focus on grantseeking approaches aimed at specific publics: government funders, private foundations, the business and professional communities (the private sector), and voluntary organizations (such as the United Way and civic associations).

The planning and program development processes are discussed in Chapter 9. It is followed by step-by-step instructions on proposal writing in Chapter 10. The next chapter continues with instructions or preparing budgets and on their use for program design and for accountability purposes. You will need to show potential suppliers that you know where the expenditure of money will do the most good and that you can make do with other resources when funds are in short supply. In the final chapter we will explore what to do after you have submitted a proposal, how to deal with a rejection, and how to swing into action if you are funded.

All but Chapter 1 include exercises for you to complete independently or with colleagues. They are intended to enable you to build the analytic and interactional skills necessary to succeed at program design and grantsmanship. You will be able to compare your experiences with those of the many seasoned practitioners whose efforts are recorded throughout the book. I have quoted them directly, allowing them to speak for themselves. Although some follow approaches that have proven themselves over the years, others describe new methods that may not yet have appeared elsewhere in the literature. Many of their successes can be replicated elsewhere, but do not accept their suggestions uncritically. Several of the persons I have quoted are not all that successful. Others may have been involved in activities that will have little relevance to your situation. Do not just read for techniques. Look for the practice principles that will apply broadly, those that you are comfortable with, and those that you can learn from.

CASTING A WIDE NET

"Money," as the expression goes, "is the root of all evil." Not true. First of all, that is a misquote. The proper quote is, "the *love* of money is the root of all evil," and by that is meant its worship, its elevation to idolatrous proportions. Money is a commodity, a resource, a means to achieve objectives that are important and meaningful. You and your organization will have to decide what is important and meaningful, and for whom.

You will also have to decide on the sources of supply you wish to tap: the government, the voluntary sector, the private sector, individual donors, or the persons who pay a fee for service. The wider the net you cast and the more varied the waters in which to troll, the less dependent you will be on a single source, and the greater likelihood that when one source dries up, others will be available from which to draw.

However, do not think of fund raising in the same way we usually think of a fishing expedition. The objective is not to drop a line in the water to see what you can hook. The objective is to get the resources you need and to put them to effective use. That will require a carefully planned and targeted approach to grantsmanship and to other fund-raising activities.

Throughout the text I will be using terminology that may be new to you. Why not turn to the glossary in Appendix A? Become familiar with the terms we will be using. Initially, they may provoke more questions than they answer. Keep those questions in mind as you read on. You will find the answers in the text and in the experiences of others with whom you interact at work.

Appendix B provides you with a number of suggestions about where you can go for additional information. Although the appendix is limited, the book is not. You will find additional resources discussed in the text of each chapter and in the suggestions for further readings that follow each summary statement.

Good fishing!

Chapter 2

ASSESSING YOUR PROGRAM'S MARKETABILITY

VIGNETTE 2: GOING TO BAT FOR THE DYING

Marylou was 39 when she died. Our children were 16 and 14. It took her six months to die; two in the hospital, but the last, at our insistence, at home. Her death wasn't an easy one; cancer patients don't generally have an easy time of it. It wasn't made any easier by the disapproval we had to deal with for bringing her home.

It happens that I am a medical social worker and that I am employed by the hospital in which she was being treated. I have had a lot of experience working with dying patients and their families. I had always thought that the saddest part of dying was dying alone. As caring as the nursing staff at the hospital might be, a hospital is still a hospital. Dying may be toughest on family members. They seem never to get the chance of "finishing their business" with a loved one; of saying all the things that need saying. Hospitals just aren't the right environment for it.

That's why Marylou came home. She had business of her own to finish and she wanted the kids to come to terms and to understand, and to do and say what they had to, no holds barred, and no guilt later on.

One of the hardest parts of it for me was dealing with some of my colleagues and especially the medical staff at the hospital. It wasn't just suspicion; it was outright hostility. I was accused of being over-emotional and not accepting reality, even of being unprofessional. There were a number of subtle hints suggesting that I might not be fit for hospital work any more. It made me angry. You get that way when you are about to lose someone you love and when someone else tells you how you should deal with that loss. So I decided to fight back.

When one of our local newspaper reporters asked if they could interview us, Marylou and I decided it would be a good idea. The kids agreed. We told our story and why we had decided that home was the best place to die. The paper printed it. The amount of response from people we had never heard of, and from some of my former clients, and even from some of our friends who had not understood before, well, it was overwhelming.

"Do something with it," Marylou told me a few days before she died. "Use our experience to help other people take charge of their own dying."

Trying to change things at the hospital, considering the attitudes there, didn't seem like the place to start. I've always believed in building on strength, and the strength seemed to be in the sentiments of all those who had given us encouragement. For several months after Marylou died, the kids and I spoke to any group that invited us: churches, the local PTA at the high school the girls attended, a chapter of the AARP [American Association of Retired Persons], even people in their own homes who invited friends and relatives to attend.

I had by this time read of Dr. Cicely Saunders' experiment at St. Christopher's in London. It was the beginning of what has since come to be known as the hospice movement. Dr. Saunders was on a speaking tour in this country. By now we had organized a committee for Being At Home, and a number of influential people were willing to "go to BAT" for the right of a patient to spend his or her last days at home or in a homelike environment.

More than two hundred people came to hear Dr. Saunders at the Presbyterian church. The press was there, and we arranged to have TV coverage and two radio interviews for her while she was in town. We recorded the talk and made it available to the community college radio station for airing some time in the future.

That was the start of it. Public opinion was strongly behind us and BAT established several task groups. This was in 1973 and the Connecticut Hospice at Yale was by then a year or two old. We delegated some people to visit and learn about their operation. We organized a health professional's task force, small at first, to look for support in the medical community. An ecumenical group organized to explore the possibilities of a general fund-raising campaign. They decided to begin by working with their own congregants and parishioners on fund raising within the churches and synagogues. They also recruited volunteers and so did the AARP and a fledgling Grey Panther group.

Several social workers, nurses, and I set up a training program for volunteers and for anyone who wanted to care for a dying patient at home. We involved others who had had experiences like mine. A small grant from a local pharmaceutical manufacturer helped with mailing. We used an empty office in one of the churches. But we didn't have the kinds of funds we would really need nor a real organization yet.

When contributions began coming in from the churches and synagogues and from private, unsolicited donations, we decided to incorporate BAT. One of the social workers on the board worked for the public welfare department and laid out the range of possibilities for support through Medicare, Medicaid, Title XX of the Social Security Act, which is administered by the State Department of Public Welfare, and Title III of the Older Americans Act of 1973 (it had just been passed).

The chair of the new Area Agency on Aging Advisory Council was also on our board. She pushed for putting BAT on the list of potential recipients for Title III funds. Our fund raisers were also on the lookout for a facility we might use for those people who could not return home but wished to die in a homelike environment. An estate attorney active in one of the churches came through for us. We had a house, if we could bring it up to code and staff it. It took another year to be able to do that.

BAT became a fully operational hospice in 1975. We help about 800 people a year, work with more than 150 volunteers, have a professional staff of 60. Our funds come from the state and federal governments, the United Fund, and our own endowment program as well as several fund-raising events each year. We also charge our consumers on the basis of their ability to pay. One day of hospice care runs about $40. Compare that to $400 or more for a hospital room.

Our board is made up of lay people, health care, and other professional people. And while money is always an issue, today, 10 years after we incorporated, public support no longer is. We are affiliated with the National Hospice Organization in Vienna, Virginia, and through that with over 400 hospices throughout the country.

We now operate a 37-bed facility although many patients are helped to stay at home or to live with relatives and friends. Treatment begins with a home visit or a visit in the hospital if that is when we are first approached. A hospice team made up of nurses, doctors, social workers, and volunteers then provides service on a 24-hour basis. The team is usually coordinated by a nurse. But we don't stop here.

We also do follow-up with members of the family after a patient has died and may refer them to other agencies, attorneys, and so on. We also do a lot of public education. Our staff and volunteers make frequent addresses to church and synagogue groups, to civic and professional associations. And we do a lot of consciousness raising and training with the staffs of hospitals and other health and social agency personnel.

GETTING IN POSITION

Those of you who may have been involved in efforts to establish a local hospice program, or for that matter, any service alternative or any kind of service expansion, will find familiar elements in the BAT example. It took several years before a hospice could be established. Many elements had to be in position first. "Positioning" required getting support of various publics, including potential consumers and funders. And it required both public *recognition of a need* and *acceptance of the approach* to be used to meet that need.

In general, positioning requires being in the right place at the right time and having the capacity to respond to opportunities when they present themselves. It may also require creating the opportunities when they do not. A good idea will not get very far if no one is ready to listen to it, it there are no resources to put it into effect, or if no one is willing to support it. Finally, getting into position requires access to the right publics.

All organizations must be able to manage relationships to three kinds of publics: those that provide inputs, those that transform inputs into products or services, and those that consume those outputs. Let us examine each of these publics one at a time.

INPUT PUBLICS AND
THE RESOURCES THEY SUPPLY

Input publics include all those that supply an organization with needed resources and with the legitimacy to do something with those resources. Resources include concrete items such as money, facilities, and equipment and such ephemerals as expertise, political influence, and energy.

Money is supplied by government agencies, voluntary organizations such as the United Way, philanthropic foundations, business organizations, and corporate givers and by individual donors who contribute to campaigns and special fund-raising events. Finally, it is supplied by consumers who pay fees to cover part or all of the cost of service.

Facilities and equipment can be purchased with money, but they can also be contributed by other organizations, as in the example of the church that donated office space to BAT in its early days. Individuals might also contribute facilities and equipment in the form of private contributions.

Expertise is found in public or voluntary sector organizations such as universities, libraries, and professional journals or books published by the public, private, and voluntary sectors. It is also found in an organization's staff, in the volunteers who work with the organization or for it, and among consultants that may be available to the organization on a time-limited basis. Sometimes the same organization that provides financial support through grants, contracts, or purchase-of-service agreements also contributes expertise through technical assistance.

Political influence may be generated through association with powerful publics and through their involvement in program development and design. *Energy* also comes from all these publics. It requires a commitment and a willingness to invest time and creativity in the program and resource development processes. Finally, *legitimacy* refers to the consensus that what the organization has set out to do — and how it does it and for whom — is considered appropriate. Agencies are dependent for their legitimacy on a variety of sources.

It is not enough, for example, that an organization to be legitimated by a board of directors or a citizen's advisory committee if funding sources do not consider the service to be legitimate. Nor is legitimacy provided by the suppliers of resources sufficient if consumers do not perceive the organization to be legitimate. Well-meaning agencies have all too frequently attempted to provide services to ethnic minorities that see the organization as representing a hostile and controlling society.

Exercise 2.1 will provide you with an opportunity to inventory the suppliers of an organization you are familiar with. Take a few moments to complete it before going on to an examination of the agency's throughput and output publics. Complete it by yourself or with colleagues in the organization you are assessing. You may find their input necessary to get accurate information. You may also find that doing it with others stimulates new ideas on where to go for additional resources.

INSTRUCTIONS FOR EXERCISE 2.1
INVENTORY OF INPUT PUBLICS

(1) Look over the Input Publics Matrix. Think of an organization you are familiar with: a social agency, a school, a hospital, and so on. Begin by identifying all the suppliers of financial resources and list these next to the appropriate row in the first column. For the hospice example described in the vignette, you might list Medicare, Medicaid, the Area Agency on Aging, and the Department of Public Welfare next to Government Agencies. Next to Voluntary Associations, you would list the various churches and synagogues and the United Way. The pharmaceutical company would be identified next to Private Sector Organizations. The publics solicited for individual funds and categories of consumers from whom donations and fees were collected would be listed next. Now complete the matrix for each of the other resource categories: facilities and equipment, expertise, political influence, energy, and legitimacy.

You may find that some organizations or groups appear more than once under several headings or in several rows. What does this suggest to you?

Be as complete as you can. Check with others if your information is limited.

(2) Now go back to each supplier you identified. If you think that it could be tapped for a significant increase in allocations, circle it in a different color pen or pencil.

(3) Finally, go back to the matrix again. In the second color, add new supplier publics that the organization is not currently tapping but that are potentially significant contributors.

(4) What might be done to increase contributions of needed resources from those suppliers identified in the Input Publics Worksheet? Jot down some preliminary ideas on a separate sheet of paper.

You will have occasion to refer back to both worksheets in completing exercises in subsequent chapters.

Exercise 2.1
INPUT PUBLICS MATRIX

Publics	Resources					
	Money	Equipment/ Facilities	Expertise	Political Influence	Time/ Energy	Legitimacy
Government Agencies						
Voluntary Organizations						
Foundations						
Private Sector Organizations						
Individual Donors						
Consumers						

OUTPUT PUBLICS

Let us turn our attention now to the organization's output publics; those that make up the consumers of its products or services. This is what is often referred to as the organization's *market*. In the example of the BAT Hospice, individuals and families who use the hospice for residence, counseling, or instruction are clearly consumers. But what of the members of churches and synagogues, or the hospital's medical personnel, who also receive training or new insights from the hospice staff?

Output publics may also include other organizations: those that receive direct services from the first organization and those that may receive referrals of clients. Who are your organization's output publics? Are some more central to the organization's missions than others? Are some targeted for special attention? For example, let us assume that you are employed by a community mental health center. Does the center provide services to everyone in the community, or are the center's services targeted to specific populations? If so, it may have planned to engage in a process of "market segmentation."

Market segmentation refers to a process whereby the market is divided into fairly homogeneous parts such that one or more can be targeted for recruitment or specialized services. The market can be segmented geographically, functionally, demographically, or psychographically. *Geographic* segmentation refers to the locale(s) in which service takes place. It can be drawn up on the basis of size, density, or both. In my home state of Michigan, for example, some community mental health centers serve multiple-county rural areas covering thousands of square miles. Others serve densely populated neighborhoods or clusters of neighborhoods in the Detroit area. The term "catchment area" generally refers to geographic segmentation.

Functional segmentation refers to the way in which services are clustered around given problems: for example, housing, job counseling, protective services, family treatment, and the like. *Demographic* segmentation may be used to target populations by age, race or ethnic identity, religion, national origin, gender, income, education, life cycle, type of employment, and so on. *Psychographic* characteristics are somewhat more subtle. They include such variables as personality, lifestyle, commitment to the organization, and even readiness to use a service.

In the case of the mental health center we have been considering, the market may have been segmented to serve a particular neighborhood. Services may be aimed primarily at teenagers and their parents, particularly if the teens are actual or potential substance abusers. Separate programs may be set up for males and for females. A decision may have been made to work with Black youngsters first because there is a readiness among members of the community to take responsibility for both treatment and prevention (psychographic characteristic = readiness).

In the case of the hospice described earlier, can you identify its market segment from the information provided? What else would you need to know? Now it is your turn to do a market segmentation analysis on an organization with which you are familiar, or a particular work unit within it.

EXERCISE 2.2
MARKET SEGMENTATION ANALYSIS

(1)   Start by describing the general geographic area that your organization serves. Now pinpoint it more precisely. For example, the general area may be the northwest suburbs, but you may attempt to recruit most heavily from a particular subarea, or perhaps residents of one or more areas have come to see your organization as the place to go for service, even if you would like to draw from a larger area. Use the Market Segmentation Matrix for recording purposes.

(2)   Now do the same for each of the other variables: functional, demographic, and psychographic.

(3)   Go over your categories in a second color of ink or pencil, circling those items that require modification.

(4)   Now add the segmentation characteristics of populations your organization is not serving, is underserving but *should* be serving in, the second color.

(5)   What should be done to increase the likelihood that the organization will be able to serve those populations it should be serving? Record your preliminary ideas on a separate sheet of paper.

You will have opportunities to refer back to this exercise as you progress through the book.

Exercise 2.2
MARKET SEGMENTATION MATRIX

Method of Segmentation	General Population	Specific Segment Within It
Geographic		
Functional		
Demographic		
Psychographic		

INTERNAL PUBLICS

Input and output publics are external to the organization. Throughout publics are *internal*; they transform resources into products (outcomes and services) that are consumed by output publics. These persons include paid and volunteer staff, members of advisory committees, task groups, and boards. Throughput publics may also be consumers involved in the provision of their own services. Some consumer/providers may be organized, as in the case of unions or other collective bargaining units, professional associations, and self-help groups.

The extent to which your organization will be able to *attract resources* from its input publics is likely to be influenced by the reputation, the competence, and the energy of these internal publics. The extent to which they will be able to turn *resources into products* will depend on how they are organized, the kinds of knowledge and skill they possess, and their perspectives of what should be done as well as their commitments to doing it. The extent to which they will be able to *attract consumers* will be based on the same variables. Are there other characteristics that are equally important?

Should internal publics reflect the demographics of the consumer population (perhaps in such characteristics as gender, marital status, and ethnicity)? Should their skills be general, as in counseling, or should they be specific to the functions that they perform in the organization (e.g., substance abuse counseling or counseling battered wives)? Should they reflect certain desirable psychographic characteristics such as commitment to the organization or to its consumers, a shared ideological or ethical perspective, or an ability to be flexible in the way in which they organize their work hours or apply intervention techniques? Does the organization require that staff and board members live in the same geographic area as do consumers?

Time for another exercise.

EXERCISE 2.3
INTERNAL PUBLICS IDENTIFICATION

(1) Look over the matrix. You will have to do a bit more on this one than on the matrixes for Exercises 2.1 and 2.2. This matrix is only partly constructed. You will have to fill in the numbers under each of the four categories. For example, if there are geographic restrictions on the employment of staff or the involvement of volunteers who perform any numbers of tasks from direct service to fund raising to policy making, jot down these instructions or requirements next to the numbers in the space to the left.

Do the same for demographic characteristics like age, gender, and so on. Then do it for functional requirements. These might be defined in terms of knowledge (e.g. *knowledge* about the community, or *knowledge* about child placement practice); skill (for example, skill in behavior modification or in proposal writing campaign management); and degree or certification requirements, if any (MSW or ACSW or state license). If you do not have enough space, make yourself a larger matrix.

Now do the same for psychographic characteristics such as commitment to the organization, identity with a particular ethnic or cultural community, willingness to assume responsibility for others, and so forth.

You may find it easier to complete this column after you have identified the staff and volunteers in the uppermost row. Staff might include direct service workers, managers, specialists, and consultants. Volunteers may include those who provide direct services, who train or supervise others, who raise funds, who perform specialized tasks such as accounting or legal advice, and who are involved in program development and decision making (like members of committees, task forces, and boards).

Once you have identified all the paid and volunteer publics, indicate which of the required characteristics are needed by checking the appropriate space in the columns to the right of each characteristic.

(2) Now, using a second color, circle those characteristics in the column under each of the identified publics that require some modification.

(3) If new categories of volunteers or paid staff should be added, add them in your second color on the uppermost row and fill in the required characteristics in the second color.

(4) Jot down notes an a separate piece of paper on how you or the organization might achieve a more desirable mix of paid and volunteer staff.

Keep your notes. We'll be referring to them again shortly.

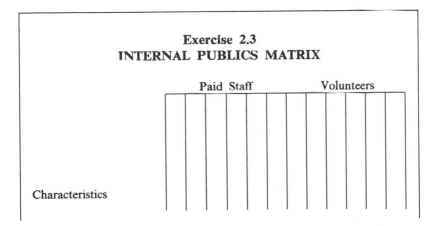

Exercise 2.3
INTERNAL PUBLICS MATRIX

Paid Staff   Volunteers

Characteristics

(Continued)

Geographic
   Requirements:
   1.
   2.
   3.
   4.
   5.
   6.
   7.
   8.

Demographic
   Requirements:
   1.
   2.
   3.
   4.
   5.
   6.
   7.
   8.

Functional
   Requirements:
   1.
   2.
   3.
   4.
   5.
   6.
   7.
   8.

Psychographic
   Requirements:
   1.
   2.
   3.
   4.
   5.
   6.
   7.
   8.

MATCHING PUBLICS

Once you have identified your key publics, the marketing challenge is to match them in such a way as to optimize your fund-raising and grantsmanship potential. Which of your consumer populations is a funding organization (e.g., an Area Agency on Aging or a State Department of Mental Hygiene) going to be most concerned about? In presenting your case to that organization, to what extent will the characteristics of your staff and the extensiveness of volunteer involvement be arguments in your favor? What must you say about them in order to present the most convincing argument?

Will volunteers with certain psychographic characteristics be induced to work on behalf of an agency perceived to serve clients with different characteristics? Middle-income volunteers might be induced to raise funds on the behalf of the deserving poor, for example, those who have been victimized by the economy; they may not be willing to work as hard for consumers who are perceived as shiftless, unmotivated, or unresponsive. They might be even less motivated to work on behalf of persons who are geographically distant although this is not necessarily the case. Geographic distance and the mystique attached to it may be a factor in generating large contributions. Witness the various Vietnam relief efforts of the late 1970s and the ongoing support for Israel by American Jews.

Paid staff, too, will require certain characteristics to work with volunteers, with funders, and with consumer groups. The characteristics required to work with one set of publics may not be adequate to work with another.

For example, in the hospice case, physicians were found more effective than others in negotiating support and referrals from hospitals. Influential older persons were effective in generating grants from the area agency, particularly when they could back up the request with evidence of competent professional personnel at the hospice. Persons who had themselves made use of the hospice were among the most effective solicitors in a communitywide telephone campaign.

Just as some publics will be drawn to each other — for example, a government funding source may be drawn to an agency that has demonstrated extensive local support from the voluntary and private sectors — others may be turned off by the presence of certain characteristics or by their absence. "You've got only two Hispanics on your staff of 33, and not a single resident from the barrio on your board. How can you expect to understand us? Why should we come to you for service?" "We cannot approve your request for funding. Although we appreciate the desirability of community involvement in the self-help process, the regulations governing allocation of funds through grants and contracts require evidence of professional competence in the delivery of services. Should you decide to reapply in the future, you might consider . . . "

ESTABLISHING PARTNERSHIPS WITH KEY PUBLICS

The kind of commitment you can expect from various publics will depend on the stake they have in your organization's success. And that stake is likely to be increased by the extent to which that success is translated into their own successes. Let me explain. In order to discharge its mandate, a federal agency may be as interested in finding the right local service organization to fund as your organization is to get the cash it needs to operate. A corporation is likely to see its contribution to your organization as effective Public relations, and perhaps as a way of maximizing profits. As we will see in Chapter 5, some insurance companies have funded local neighborhood organizations in hopes of stabilizing those neighborhoods, and in so doing have reduced the numbers of claims for thefts, accidents, or health benefits.

Other service organizations, too, may be turned from output or input publics into co-equal partners. The nature of the partnership depends on how the exchanges between organizations are perceived. For example, when hospitals or private physicians refer patients to the hospice, they may view the hospice as an output public, whereas the hospice may view the referral organizations as input publics. The relationships between the two may be formal and without too much commitment. Each may perceive the relationship as a way of better serving a mutual client. A referring physician may see the hospice as a resource to be used in his or her practice, a resource that enhances that practice and with it his or her professional reputation and repertoire. The hospice may perceive the physician as an important source of information and legitimacy; its staff and volunteers may invest in that relationship accordingly.

One form of exchange, referrals, for example, may lead to a variety of others. On the following pages you will find an inventory of interagency exchange mechanisms that link agencies in partnership relationships. Look it over, and then complete your own inventory of linking mechanisms on the form provided for Exercise 2.4. A more extensive discussion of linking mechanisms can be found in Rossi et al. (1981), described at the end of this chapter.

INSTRUCTIONS FOR EXERCISE 2.4
INVENTORY OF POTENTIALLY USEFUL LINKING MECHANISMS

(1) Look over the inventory of possible linking mechanisms between service organizations. Check all those that your organization currently uses with one or more other service providers, and others if they apply.

(2) In a different color, circle those numbers that require more work and check those that are not currently in use but should be.

(3) On the Linking Mechanism Worksheet, list all the linking mechanisms operating between your organization and another service provider. What could be done to increase the range of linkages? How might these increase your organization's marketability with other input and output publics? To what extent might it reduce your need for funds or increase your access to them?

Again, we will be referring to your notes later on.

Exercise 2.4
INVENTORY OF POTENTIALLY USEFUL LINKING MECHANISMS

A. MEETING IMMEDIATE CLIENT NEEDS

__ 1. Cross-Referrals
__ 2. Case Consultation
__ 3. Case Conferences
__ 4. Client Teams
__ 5. Case Management
__ 6. Joint Intake, Screening, Diagnosis
__ 7. Case Management by One Agency
__ 8. _____
__ 9. _____
__ 10. _____

B. MEETING AGENCY PERSONNEL NEEDS

__ 1. Staff Outstationing
__ 2. Co-Location of Staff
__ 3. Loaner Staff Arrangements
__ 4. Joint Training and Staff Development
__ 5. _____
__ 6. _____
__ 7. _____

C. GATHERING, EXCHANGING, AND DISSEMINATING IN-
FORMATION
   — 1. Joint Community Needs Assessment or Special Studies
   — 2. Information Clearinghouse
   — 3. Joint Data Gathering or Management Information System
   — 4. Joint Program Evaluation
   — 5. Interorganizational Consultation or Technical Assistance
   — 6. Joint Public Relations, News Releases, and Community
       Education
   — 7. _____
   — 8. _____
   — 9. _____

D. INTEGRATING PROGRAMS AND ADMINISTRATION
   — 1. Joint Standards and/or Guidelines
   — 2. Sharing Facilities and/or Equipment
   — 3. Joint Program Design
   — 4. Joint Program Operation
   — 5. Purchases of Service
   — 6. Joint Budgeting
   — 7. Joint Fund-Raising
   — 8. Joint Funding (Allocation)
   — 9. Standardized Proceedures
   — 10. _____
   — 11. _____
   — 12. _____

Exercise 2.4
LINKING MECHANISM WORKSHEET

Name another service organization with which your organization is
regularly involved: _____
List the range of linkages currently in place between them.

_____   _____
_____   _____
_____   _____
_____   _____
_____   _____
_____   _____

What others might be added? Add them in a different color.
How might you induce the other organization to engage in a wider variety of exchanges with yours?

What changes in the way in which your internal publics work might be necessary? What inducements are necessary? What kinds of supports?

What are the implications for funding, for other resources, and for your relationships to various resource suppliers?

What are the implications for your relationship to current consumers or to potential consumer publics?

DEVELOPING A MARKETING STRATEGY

If you have completed these exercises, you are well on your way to developing a marketing strategy. Marketing refers to the development of relationships to various publics that provide the organization with the resources it needs and/or that consume its products. Strategic marketing is aimed at increasing demand for the agency's products among both consumers and suppliers. Successful strategic marketing requires the internal capacity to deliver what is promised. So far, we have explored one of the *P*s of the marketing process — *publics* and the ways in which publics can be turned into *partners*. There are four other *P*s: *products, price, place,* and *promotions.* I will take them up one at a time.

PRODUCTS, PRICE, PLACE, AND PROMOTIONS

Products are the organization's services and the outcomes of those services. For example, the hospice's services include counseling, nursing care, medical treatment, and so on. The intended outcome for patients is a more humane way to die, and for their families, the hospice's outcome is a reduction in guilt and in associated trauma. People may be willing to buy the agency's services because they anticipate the outcome will be worth the investment cost. The same would hold true for voluntary recipients of any agency service: adoptions and foster care, job training and placement, family treatment, compensatory education, and so on. Even involuntary recipients may be willing to pay because the cost of not receiving services may be greater than receiving them. In the case of a court referral, for example, refusing service may result in a jail sentence or fine.

Other publics may be willing to pay for all or part of the product, even though they will not be direct recipients of the organization's services. These are the supplier publics we spoke of who may be mandated by law to fund certain programs through contracts and grants, and who may see it as advantageous to have someone else perform tasks they are not capable of assuming directly. Some have altruistic, religious, and ideological commitments to certain services as they do to populations in need. Remember that the resources supplied need not be money alone. Other resources include facilities, equipment, energy, technical expertise, and political influence.

Your organization's products will be shaped by the willingness of some publics to consume them, others to supply the necessary resources, and still others to turn those resources into products.

The *price* is what each of these publics is willing to pay. The price may be in dollars: dollars awarded in grants, allocated in yearly appropriations, raised in a "bricks and mortar" drive, paid in fees for services received, donated in response to a telephone campaign. Payment can be made in-kind through the donation or allocation of facilities or supplies, through allocation of volunteer time, or to tasks that might otherwise cost your organization money. But there are more than dollar costs to be concerned about.

There are also *social* costs, *psychological* costs, and *opportunity* costs. When volunteers contribute two evenings a week to the hospice, they may be giving up customary bridge games, family time, or other opportunities to socialize. When a funding agency commits itself to your organization, it may be making a social commitment by identifying itself as your organization's sponsor. When local leaders agree to serve on your organization's board or capital campaign cabinet, they are committing not only their time but their prestige to your organization.

Psychological costs are the things one may have to give up in terms of personal image and sense of self, or the stresses one must endure in order to gain other anticipated benefits. Working with dying patients is painful for both staff and volunteers. Making an emotional commitment to a neighborhood association may require taking risks one might not have been ready for only a few months earlier. Applying for service to a family agency may require admitting that one is not capable, at least for the moment, to deal with one's problem without outside help. And it may require at least a partial dependence on the helper or helping system. Working on a demonstration project may require agency staff to work long hours and to undergo stressful periods of uncertainty as a new program is put into practice.

Opportunity costs do not refer to what is paid out in money, time and energy, supplies, psychological commitment, and so on, but to what might have been gained from making those commitments elsewhere. Thus, when the United Way allocates $250,000 to your organization, it is left with a quarter of a million dollars less to allocate elsewhere. When a client enters a job-training program under Goodwill Industries' auspices, he or she may have to give up the opportunity of seeking training or employment elsewhere, at least for the duration of the training.

Dollar costs are only a part of what suppliers and consumers may be asked to pay. Other costs may be much more significant. Once having committed themselves to pay in one way, it may be much easier to induce various publics to support the organization in other ways. Thus, if the Area Agency on Aging or the United Way planning staff have been involved in helping to design a particular program or service, and is satisfied that your organization can be held accountable for those services, it may be willing to allocate the necessary funds.

In most of the marketing literature, the term "place" refers to the distribution of goods and services. Again, the hospice example provides an interesting illustration of how services can be transformed, reduced in cost, and made more effective by being relocated from one facility to another. In this case, however, relocation also required a new auspice, in fact, the establishment of a new organization with both the commitments and the technology to provide the service. Neither funding nor legitimacy were at first available. These had to be developed through a promotional campaign. Before we move on to promotions, it may be helpful to examine some other connotations of place.

The word "place" can refer to the importance of a particular funder in an agency's support system, or the place that the organization plays in the funder's output system. For example, if there are many group-home facilities available, and a relatively modest supply of youngsters in need of protective care in a community setting, then the *place* of a particular group home in the array of potential contractors for the state welfare department may not be very secure. But if there is a great need for group homes, and no others are available in a particular community, the group home may be in a very secure financial position. It may be able to *place* demands on the state agency for special consideration and for the resources needed to expand its facilities and its services.

The word "place" can also refer to the place in an organization's development: the organization's readiness to take on a new service program, to modify existing practices, to seek new sources of funding and other support.

It can refer to the place in a person's "life space," the importance a particular service or activity may have to the person at a specific time in his or her life or career. For example, an outreach worker may not be ready to take on a fund-raising task until he or she has developed confidence in his or her competence and knowledge of the substantive area for which funds are being sought.

What place does the service program for which you have responsibility hold in the life or organization space of its various external publics — such as funders, potentially collaborating service organizations, and consumers — and its internal publics like staff and volunteers?

That place can be made more visible and more secure through effective *promotions.* Promotional activity can be aimed at selling a particular product, raising public consciousness, or properly positioning your organization and its products for new or expanded relationships with targeted publics. Selling a product, in human service terms, requires informing targeted publics that the product is available, where, and at what cost. It also requires informing the public of the benefits of using a particular product. At first blush, this may seem overly commercial, not the kind of thing that a human service organization does or ought to do.

But we do it all the time. Libraries advertise the availability of their bookmobiles or special reading services to the disabled. Museums inform the public of special shows or of the benefits of membership. Agencies interested in reaching new publics may dispatch staff to speaking engagements and outstationed positions in other host organizations. Press releases or feature stories on special services or seasonal programs such as summer camps are not uncommon. Some agencies even advertise clients, as in the case of those seeking to find adoptive families for hard-to-place children. What kind of selling activities did the promoters of BAT engage in? What publics did they target?

Consciousness-raising is of a slightly different order. It is not aimed at increasing demand for a particular program or product. It is aimed at increasing the likelihood that there will be support for the program or demand for it when such support or demand is needed. The general population is likely to be indifferent about the things that concern your organization: a service it provides, a population in need, or a problem to be addressed. Most people do not become interested in hospice services or adoptions until they become aware of a personal need or until they become conscious of the needs and concerns of others.

When agencies seek to promote services for unwed mothers, teenage substance abusers, or the victims of domestic violence, they often find that public awareness or receptivity to be so minimal as to preclude any possibility of adequate support. Because these issues often offend the public and challenge our images of ourselves as a society, there is often resistance to dealing with these problems. For this reason, consciousness-raising, the building of awareness and concern, may have to precede efforts to promote a particular product.

Consciousness-raising activities can be directed at particular publics: a foundation from whom support may be sought now or in the future; the Area Agency on Aging from which technical assistance may be solicited first, and funding at a future date; teens who may need family planning services now or in the near future; members of a religious community who may not only need hospice services for themselves, but may be in the position of referring others, raising money, or donating volunteer time.

Promotional activities can take many forms. Partners in the process may include the local press, TV and radio stations, or the many social agencies, civic associations, and professional groups found in any community. The press features news articles, regular columns, and advertisements. Similar content may be carried in agency newsletters in corporate house organs, church or civic group newsletters, and so on. TV and radio might also be used for news releases. Public service announcements are another possibility. So are interviews and participation in talk and phone-in shows. Public appearances and community education programs also promote program and services, as do one-on-one personal contacts and relationships. Which of these approaches does your organization use on a regular basis?

DOING WHAT YOU OUGHT TO:
APPROACHES TO ASSESSING MARKETS
AND MARKETABILITY

If you have completed the exercises in this chapter, you will have begun the assessment process of your organization and its program's marketability. In subsequent chapters you will also have the opportunity of further assessing your organization and key elements in its environment around issues of price, place, and promotions. The assessment process also focuses on needs for programs on problems that can be addressed through agency programs and services.

Assessment questions may be focused on populations, on management or resources, or on the relationships between them. When they focus on populations, either individually or collectively, questions may be asked about *debilitating attitudes, knowledge,* or *skill and capacity.* These questions can be asked of consumers, of staff and volunteers, or of resource suppliers.

Is a lack of consumer participation in job training, substance abuse counseling, or in family planning due to lack of knowledge about the availability of services and of what these services might provide them? Or is a lack of participation based on debilitating attitudes; the feeling that nothing they do will make any difference, or that the providers of service would not understand them anyway? Is it based on lack of skill in defining their problems or in presenting them in such a way as to make them comprehensible to a professional helper? Similar questions can be asked of agency staff and potential volunteers.

In considering resources and management concerns, are the sources of funding, such as government agencies and foundations, aware of what your organization does? Of the severity of the problems that the agency attempts to address at the local level? Funders, too, can suffer from debilitating attitudes, as when they refuse to examine a request from an agency because of a bias against grassroots efforts such as those of BAT. They may not possess the skills to communicate effectively with some groups because of cultural or ideological differences and perhaps even language difficulties.

When assessment focuses on resources, three sets of questions may be asked. How *available* are they and from whom? Even if they are available, are they *accessible*, or must a petitioner overcome enormous hurdles to find out what is available, how to apply, or where to submit the application? Are the resources *sufficient* to make a difference, or must sources of supply be sought from additional suppliers? Ask these questions in relation to funds, facilities, expertise, energy, and legitimacy.

When the relationship between populations and organizations and the resources they might supply are examined together, you might ask questions regarding *consistency, continuity,* and *comprehensiveness.* What is the likelihood that the same resources will be available next year or from year to year? Are the funder's resources available on a consistent basis or are priorities likely to shift without forewarning? Are funds, once allocated, likely, to be available on a continuous basis, or is the grant award only for a start-up activity?

Comprehensiveness refers to the extent to which different resources are available in sufficient quantity to complement each other. For example, although funds may be available to provide a given service, if the expertise required to conduct service activities is not, or if staff and volunteer energy is low, the funds may have little bearing on the agency's success. Resources must be properly orchestrated, each complementing the other, for a program to be successful. Sometimes, one resource, such as facilities and in-kind services, can be substituted for another resource, such as money; but if the right mix cannot be brought together in some comprehensive manner, the resultant program is likely to be less than was hoped for.

These can be treated as *here-and-now* types of issues that focus on *what is.* In *anticipatory* assessment one asks the same kinds of questions, but the focus is on the extent to which these problems are likely to be felt in the future. For example, one might make projections on the basis of anticipated or unanticipated changes. What might be the likely drain on existing services should unemployment double or triple in the next five years? Would one wish, then, to focus on the debilitating attitudes of our clients or on their lack of marketable skills? Or, assuming current trends and the completion of the legislation processes aimed at shifting responsibilities from the public to the private sector, and from federal to state and local jurisdictions, to what extent might one anticipate continued problems of program availability, accessibility, accountability, effectiveness, or efficiency?

The advantages of anticipatory assessment are that it permits practitioners and program planners to think ahead rather than to catch up with problems after the fact. It enables you to make decisions now that are likely to head off problems and their consequences for the populations for which your organization is mandated to provide services.

Normative assessment begins with an image of a desired state. Ask yourself what kind of services you would like to see in place several years from now, or what kinds of capacities you would like clients, staff members, or target populations to develop. What kind of funding pattern would you like to see in place? Begin by deciding what a minimally acceptable service program might look like, perhaps in terms of such issues as availability and accessibility. In effect, what you would be doing is developing a competency model that describes the desired state of affairs.

When a planning and allocating body, such as the United Fund, establishes minimum standards for service agencies, it establishes a competency model. Professional associations and accrediting bodies such as the Child Welfare League of America and the American Hospital Association do the same. For assessment purposes, designing the model is only the first step. You would then examine where the population or the service system is now in relationship to the norms you have specified. You might do the same in relation to the funding pattern that would have to be operable in order to support the described services. It is the gap between current reality and the desired state of affairs that would direct you in your program development efforts. Once you have uncovered present levels of competency and compared them to the norms you desire, you would then specify your objectives and set priorities on the basis of salience (importance) and feasibility.

REVIEW

To be marketable, your organization must be properly positioned. Positioning requires being in the right place at the right time and having the capacity to respond to opportunities when they present themselves, or of making those opportunities. Opportunities for program development and expansion depend on relationships with various publics. Input publics provide the organization with the resources it needs to survive and to develop and deliver its products. Resources include money, facilities and equipment, expertise, political influence, energy, and legitimacy. Although sometimes one resource can be used to substitute for another, in general, an effective resources strategy requires development and orchestration of many resources from many suppliers.

Output publics include the direct and indirect consumers of an organization's products. These may be individual clients, other organizations that receive intelligence or referrals from your organization, and others who transform your outputs into their inputs. Unlike input and output publics that are external to the organization, throughput publics are internal. They include the staff, volunteers, and others who are involved in the transformation of resources into outputs through the agency's various services and programs.

Together, these publics make up the organization's markets. Markets can be segmented such that particular elements within it can be targeted for recruitment, change, service, and so on. Segmentation can be based on geographic, functional, demographic, or psychographic distinctions. The ability of an organization to reach out to consumer publics may have considerable impact on its effectiveness in reaching supplier publics and vice versa. Frequently, its capacity is based on the skill, commitment, and knowledge of its staff and volunteers.

Any of these publics are potential partners of your agency. To the extent that each of the partners sees advantages to themselves of being linked to your organization, they are likely to invest in those relationships. A number of potentially available partnership or linking mechanisms between service providers was included.

In addition to concern with various publics, an effective marketing strategy requires attention to four other words beginning with the letter *P*: *products, price, place,* and *promotions*. Products are the organization's services and the outcomes of those services. Price is the cost of services and other agency operations. The price may be shared by institutional funders like government agencies, voluntary funding organizations, philanthropic foundations, private sector organizations, and by individual donors and the consumers who pay fees for services received. But price can also refer to social, psychological, and opportunity costs, many of which can be as significant as financial costs.

Place refers to the location of an organization and its services geographically, in time, and in the life or organization space of its various publics. Your agency's ability to attract resources on a consistent and sustained basis will depend on its location in one of these dimensions. Promotion refers to the activities involved in informing relevant publics about the agency and its programs. It includes heightening public awareness and consciousness-raising as well as selling an idea, a need, or a product.

A number of approaches can be used to assess your organization's marketability. You might focus on current input, throughput, and output publics. You might also be future oriented in anticipation of what would have to be done in order to properly prepare for a set of circumstances that are likely to occur. Finally, assessment can be normative. A model of a desired state of affairs is designed, and current or anticipated situations are then compared to the normative model.

This, then, sets the stage for development of an effective market strategy.

SUGGESTIONS FOR FURTHER READING

Kotler, Philip. *Marketing for Nonprofit Organizations*. Englewood Cliffs, NJ: Prentice-Hall, 1982.
    Clear and straightforward discussion of marketing methods, market analysis, product decisions, and the establishment of a marketing organization within a nonprofit organization.

Lauffer, Armand. *Assessment Tools*. Beverley Hills, CA: Sage, 1982.
    Seven assessment tools are discussed: ecomaping, forcefield analysis, the nominal group technique, Delphi, photography, gaming, and task analysis. Instructions are given for their use in here-and-now, anticipatory, and normative assessment.

Lauffer, Armand. *Getting the Resources You Need*. Beverly Hills, CA: Sage, 1982.
    Focuses on getting the right mix of people, program, and strategic resources, including extensive treatment of interorganizational relationships.

Lauffer, Armand. *Strategic Marketing* (tentative). New York: Free Press, 1984.
    An introduction to the procedures used in making your agency and its products more marketable. Includes chapters on working with each of the organization's publics, on price, place, promotions, product design strategies and on the conduct of marketing audits.

Rossi, Robert, Gilmartin, Kevin J., and Dayton, Charles W. *Agencies Working Together*. Beverly Hills, CA: Sage, 1981.
    Step-by-step instructions for building partnership relationships between service providers and other publics.

Chapter 3

THE BUCKS START HERE
Seeking Government Funds

VIGNETTE 3: WHEN YOU'RE PLAYING
THE FUNDING GAME,
KNOW THE FUNDER'S RULES!

Here's the way I look at it: Why write a proposal unless you know in advance that you're likely to get it funded? Yes, I know there are a lot of contingencies in this game. But it's just that; it's a game. And like any game, it requires a win strategy. You sometimes lose, but it's not because you made the wrong moves. It's because there were certain things beyond your control. You can't always beat the odds, but you can make them more in your favor.

I've got a few simple rules of thumb. The first is to make sure you know what the funder wants or how to get him or her to want what you want. That requires lots of contact with the funder long before you write your final proposal. First of all, it requires finding out who is the right person to talk to. Pick up the catalogue of Domestic Federal Assistance. Check on the right program. And if you can, get a federal telephone directory to find out who the administrative officer is in a certain granting program. If you don't have the directory, call the phone number in the catalogue, or write to find out who the grants officer is for the program you are interested in. In psyching out government agencies, I find that picking up the telephone and calling the right person may be all that's needed to establish a contact. Sometimes, though, it's useful to have an introduction arranged by a friend who has had a project funded by the agency.

I've sometimes gone directly to Washington just so I might meet an official I'm anxious to build a relationship with. I've found government people pretty open to a drop-in visit or a telephone call from people in the community. Of course, drop-ins are a little risky if their schedules are tight. But still, even when money is tight the feds are pretty generally happy to see one of us community types...if we know what we are about.

Sitting off there in Washington or in a regional office can mean living in a cut-off and rarefied atmosphere. Those people need the infusion of information and insight and, I might add, a feeling of support and understanding from people out in the real world. Most of the feds realize that if they talk only to themselves, they'll fall into a rut. They're thankful to have contacts around the country. Besides, if you can give them a few facts about what kind of impact their programs are having, they use those facts as ammunition in their negotiations with higher-ups in the bureaucracy or in contacts with legislators and legislative committee staff.

Going on a "fishing" expedition does not mean going unprepared. For example, a couple of years back, I went to talk to an official of the Administration on Aging. I knew this guy was interested in self-help programs. I also knew he had a bad back. I commiserated with him over lunch about his bad back and told him I had one, too. Pretty soon we got onto home remedies, evaluations of a local surgeon we both had some dealings with, and so on. This gave me an opening to mention the use of a lay service network. He'd never heard the term before, but he caught on real fast. He told me about how he'd been part of lots of lay networks himself.

The problem as he saw it was that some people don't have access to other people who could help them. "That's right," I agreed, "especially elderly people. The older people are, the fewer contacts they have. Their friends move away, die, or become immobilized. It's just because they don't have enough family, friends, or neighbors who can help them that they're in particular need of professionalized services. But the professional services are expensive. There ought to be some way in which we can rationalize funding the lay service network in order to increase potential for self-help at the community level and reduce the drain on agency services."

Well, the guy really bit the hook on that one. Not too much later, after several preliminary drafts of a proposal, he told me to go ahead and submit the final one. Notice, I said after *the submission of preliminary proposals. I wasn't going to submit a final proposal until I knew that this was what he wanted and that he'd back us up with his review panel.*

If I can avoid it, I never submit a final proposal without first getting comments on one or more preliminary drafts. I keep those preliminary drafts short, concise, and to the point. I figure that if the feds want me to add more, they'll tell me. After all, if I fill a proposal full of garbage, they're not going to be willing to read it. So I let them tell me if they feel I've left things out.

And then I write that proposal the way the funder thinks it should be written. Usually I will ask how they want it. Sometimes a funder will say that I'm too academic in what I've written, that I should use simpler language and more illustrations. Sometimes they'll tell me that I'm too folksy, and I should make it more sophisticated in tone. Whatever they suggest, that's the way I write it.

Of course, things aren't always that easy. Sometimes you're going along real well when the funder hits you with a bombshell. Too many proposals are being submitted and your're competing with a lot of other people for a

*large share of a very small pot. Maybe there's been a cut in the
appropriation and the funder will ask you if you can do with $30,000
instead of the $80,000 you'd asked for. A time like that is when I have to
make some hard decisions. Do I let it go at that and take my chances, or
do I bring in the rest of the troops? Once when a funder called me to say
there would be less money available for my project than she had
anticipated, I pulled out a game plan that was a little bit risky.*

*First I was silent on the phone for about a minute and a half. This gave
me a chance to collect my thoughts, and it worried the woman on the
other end of the line. Then I told her I'd been silent because I knew how
difficult it must have been for her to call me, and how aware I was of
her own commitment to the program. I wanted her to know that I
understood how she felt. Then I told her how I felt. I mentioned that,
based on our previous contacts, I'd made certain promises to local people.
Several agencies were ready to get involved in the cooperative venture. I
spoke of how a lot of our local influentials were going to feel about the
project's being sliced down to one-third of our request. "What should I tell
people?" I asked. I was anxious for her to know that I was going to be
talking to our local people, and that she might get some pressure from
them. I didn't want it to come as a surprise.*

*"Tell them what you think you have to tell them," she told me, "and I'll
see what I can do from here." I thanked her for calling. Immediately I
called the chairman of my board. We figured out which local people had
the most influence with our congressman and with people in H.H.S.
[Department of Health and Human Services]. We had these people place
calls to Washington, telling them how disappointed people were at the cut
in funds and how much local support there was for the project.*

*Two days later, I got a call from my friend in Washington. "You sure
have a lot of people on your side," she said. "Submit a new budget. This
time cut it by about 25 percent. We can give you that much." Well, that
was better than cutting it by two-thirds. I thanked her and said I was
sorry if some of our local people had gotten too excited about the cut and
put the pressure on. "Well, there has been some pressure," she admitted. I
made a note to do something for her later on. A couple of weeks later, I
made sure that her superior got word from some of our local influentials
about how helpful they thought she'd been. Six months later, knowing I'd
have other dealings with her, I wrote a letter thanking her for having done
something else for us and sent a copy to her supervisor. Those little
gestures help.*

*Of course, you've got to be careful who you put the pressure on. It can
backfire, especially when you use congressmen or staff. The people in the
bureaucracy don't like to be pressured by the people on Capitol Hill. And
people on Capitol Hill don't like to be bothered with little projects. They
don't want to use up their influence on every request that comes around.
You've got to know when an issue is hot, how much resistance there'll be
toward what you want, and how much of a stake the congressman or
senator is going to have in that particular activity or in getting the funds
for his or her locality. Sometimes it's better to use a staffer in a*

congressional committee than a congressman. Staffers have their own lines to the bureaucracy.

Still, you want to be careful. Line up too many guns on your side, let it seem as if your're politicking a grant through instead of having it reviewed on its own merits, and you're likely to be dropped like a hot potato. What I mean is, know your funder and know what it takes to get a project through. If you've got a mismatch, you might as well know early and not bother.

One more word of advice. Remember that you are the petitioner. *You are the one asking for money. That can put you in a dependent position, not the best place to be if you want to be in control of your own destiny. Get yourself into a position where the funder needs you for something. Help the funder make a contact with somebody in another bureaucracy that you know well. Pass on some information that will be useful in his or her work. Some funders like to collect reprints. Invest a few dollars. Send reprints of articles that you know the person will be interested in. Indicate you ran across this in some of your work and that you thought it might be helpful.*

Don't ever let it seem that you're buying a gift. I make it a rule never *to take a potential funder out for lunch or a drink. Some feds are really uptight about those things. I once made the mistake of trying to buy a drink for a woman who works in the Office of Education. She nearly slapped me. First of all, it was a sexist thing to do. Second, she wanted to make sure she wasn't beholden to me for anything. It was different when I sent her a copy of a report on something our local community college had done that I knew would be of interest to her. She didn't interpret that as a personal favor but as a professional courtesy.*

You've got to know what rules the other person is playing by [adapted from Armand Lauffer et al., *Grantsmanship*, first edition. Beverly Hills, CA: Sage, 1977].

VIGNETTE 4: MATCHMAKING —
MAKING GRANT MONIES
WORK MORE EFFICIENTLY

Officially, I'm a grants officer and planner in the State Department of Mental Hygiene. The most exciting and probably the most important planning I do is the providing of technical assistance to local organizations and citizens' groups that apply for financial support. My particular area of expertise is in development of community placements. I don't view my technical assistance function narrowly. Some would disagree with me, but I feel it's not enough simply to help somebody to fill out the forms in proposal or project design. I think of my function as one of opening up possibilities — opening up people and agencies, as a matter of fact, to new ideas and new relationships. When I perform a technical assistance function, I think of myself as an educator, a consultant, a community developer.

*Perhaps the most significant thing I've done is to foster exchanges among
agencies and between the professional people and interested lay people in
the community. Because of my years of experience here, I know lots of
folks. I know what they're interested in. I'm sort of a broker —
matchmaker, you might call me. I match people who've got ideas in
common or problems in common.*

*Being a matchmaker is no easy task. First of all, the parties you're trying
to link up don't necessarily want to be linked up; or at least, they don't
know they want to be. Second, there is no guarantee that bringing people
together to work on a common problem is going to result in any
amelioration of the problem or in any permanent relationship. I'm getting
ahead of myself. Let me take a couple of steps back.*

*My technical assistance role begins when some agency or group approaches
the community placement officer with a project in mind or with a problem
it wants to work on, and asks specifically for some consultation or staff
assistance; or when the preliminary draft of a proposal for funding is
submitted. When someone writes or calls for a proposal packet, we send
out information indicating technical assistance on project design is
available.*

*A third possibility is that the state-level staff or one of our regional
planning councils has decided that there's some project or program it wants
to get off the ground. I take a look at the agencies and organizations in
the community that might be able to take on the project. Then I arrange
a preliminary meeting with the appropriate persons to explore the possibility
of their submitting a proposal.*

*Regardless of who initiates the contract, preliminary sessions are for getting
acquainted. Sometimes I know exactly what I want to do and what I
want to get out of the other party. But I generally don't spill the beans
right at the start. I feel out their readiness. I educate them and bring
them along until they're ready to hear what I've got to say. I give them
chances to say no before we get down to business. It works the other way,
too. Sometimes they know exactly what they want to get out of me. A
frontal attack is not always the best strategy on their part.*

*What we strive toward is a mutuality of perspective. It's like a dating
game. Each party tries to test out how far the other is willing to go until
they reach some point of accommodation. Sometimes one party is not at
all interested, in which case the other side become more aggressive or more
seductive. It's important to know where each side is coming from.*

*When I get into this testing out business, I may have a specific thing in
mind that I want the agency or organization to do; or I may want to find
out what the agency's capacity is; or I may want to help the agency to
identify what it wants to do. In the same way, the persons I'm dealing
with may already know what they want; or they may be trying to find out
what the department's priorities are and what kinds of resources we have
available; or they may just want to test themselves out against some future
possibilities. Technical assistance is like consultation. You have to know
what you have and are willing to offer and what the other side needs or
wants to get.*

One problem I've noticed with other planners is that they sometimes try to railroad something through, as if they were in some superordinate position over their constituent agencies. I think that's arrogant. I'd rather view myself as a professional helper trying to give an organization the kind of help it needs to do its job better — or, on behalf of some population that needs service, trying to help an organization change the way it does its job. It's a temporary relationship, and it should be a relationship of equals, although I know damn well that sometimes the other party's got the clout because they've got something I want. Most times I've got the clout because they want something I've got.

What I'm saying is that it's important to understand your own motivations when you're giving technical assistance, and to understand the other party's motivations in accepting it. Sometimes I'm responding because there's a call for help. At other times I'm responding because I think the system out there is unproductive, or that there are sufficient inadequacies and inefficiencies in the service system to require some change. Sometimes I get involved because I'm advocating on behalf of people that need the Office of Community Placement's help.

Whatever the motivation, the process often includes more than just the two parties initially involved. If an agency seems to need a better idea of what clients are interested in, I may arrange for meetings between the agency's administrative staff and some representatives of consumer groups such as the Greenacres Alumni Association, a self-help group of ex-mental hospital patients from the Midland area. Let's assume for a moment that the party requesting technical assistance is a psychiatric facility. I may feel that the hospital doesn't have the staff capabilities to pull off a project it is interested in. I may suggest a collaborative relationship with the community college or the department of recreation, or the Catholic family service agency.

Sometimes my technical assistance results in a project proposal. If my assistance has been useful, that proposal is going to be funded. I don't stop at project design. I may help the organization find appropriate alternative sources of funding, may make a few well-placed phone calls to open the right doors, may even help the agency locate the right staff or the right kind of help for staff retraining and retreading. And, after the project is funded, I make sure to pass on my information on the project to whomever at the state level is going to be responsible for monitoring it or providing further technical assistance [adapted from Armand Lauffer et al., *Grantsmanship*, first edition. Beverly Hills, CA: Sage, 1977].

FINDING OUT WHO'S BUYING

As both vignettes illustrate, funders and applicants both have a stake in the grants or contract award process. From the funder's perspective, good applicants and good applications are at a premium. Federal, state, or local governments agencies are mandated to support legislated programs. In the vast majority of cases, they are not able to conduct those programs with their own staff, and so are required to seek organizations and individuals that can do the government's business or through which public policy can be executed.

It may not be possible for all funders to provide the extensive technical assistance and consultation described in the second vignette, but it is highly likely that funding agencies will provide you with at least the written materials that will guide you in your proposal preparation or in seeking alternative funding sources. These materials may be extensive when supplied by federal agencies, somewhat more modest from state agencies, and minimal or nonexistent from local government sources. However, this is not always the case. The federal government has been in the grants and contracts business for a long time and has developed highly standardized procedures, but some of its agencies may be in transition or may be underfunded and understaffed. This is even more true at the state level.

State agencies are, for the most part, in a period of transition as they move to assume larger share of the responsibility for allocating tax dollars raised within the state, or for the reallocation of federal dollars. Local government sources may or may not have standardized procedures. By local government I am referring to county, city, township, or other substate districts. They will, however, tend to be more knowledgeable about local needs and may provide the most extensive technical assistance. Some local organizations, such as community development corporations, for example, are responsible for the allocation of federal and local monies to community groups and agencies. The corporation's staff may do much more than provide technical assistance. It may involve citizens in needs assessment and in plan making and then advocate on behalf of those citizens with its own board or allocations committee.

How can you find out where funds are available and for what purposes? How can you uncover what you or your organization has that a funder might be interested in supporting?

Government programs are so varied in size, scope, and style that they deserve to be the subject of another book. In fact, they have been subject of many. If you are interested in a federal award, a good book for you to begin your search with is the *Catalogue of Federal Domestic Assistance*. It is available from the Superintendent of Documents each year in May and has a fall supplement with additional supplements projected. Its price has been relatively low in recent years, but as is the case with other government publications, it is likely to skyrocket over the next decade. It can be found, however, in most public and university libraries and in the library or bookstore of your local federal building. The catalogue includes profiles of every federal funding source available to "assist Americans in furthering social and economic progress." It tells you which federal agency sponsors what programs, the legislation under which they are established, the criteria of eligibility for applicants, the deadlines for application, and the funding levels; it also provides contact names and often the telephone numbers of key officials who can provide you with additional information.

Federal agencies issue awards as contracts and as grants. Despite President Reagan's first-term efforts to distribute domestic assistance funds directly to the states in the form of block grants, most federal dollars are still administered through categorical programs; that is, there are specific categories of funds available to deal with needs and problems of various populations — such as the aging, children, or adolescents — and regions of the country. There may be subcategories of programs serving children with health needs, children with developmental disabilities, or children in need of permanent placements.

These categories sometimes overlap with problem areas such as substance abuse, chronic mental illness, hypertension, and so on. Sometimes the categories deal with such service arenas as primary or secondary education or community development. You do not need to understand the entire system to apply for funds. You only need to know which category fits the kinds of programs or services your agency is interested in. For that, the index to the *Catalogue* will be most helpful.

Some state agencies also publish catalogues. These will be available from the governor's office or from the state agencies through which programs may be funded: public welfare, health and mental health, housing, corrections, and so on. Unfortunately, the information you seek may not be so easy to uncover. If there is neither a catalogue nor some other listing, you may have to find alternative sources of information. A good place to start might be your state League for Human Services organization, the state chapter of National Association of Social Workers (NASW), or another relevant advocacy group.

Such voluntary planning bodies as the United Fund and sectarian organizations (e.g., Catholic Charities) may be in good position to point you to the appropriate state address. Their staff do more than raise funds locally and allocate them to member agencies; they also help those member agencies and others to seek funding from appropriate public sources. Consider also going to other organizations like your own: hospitals, group homes, spouse abuse shelters, and so on. Chances are that your organization is already affiliated with a public or a voluntary coordinating body — a council on aging, a community mental health board, or a coordinating council for children at risk. Who on the staff or the board of that organization can help you in your search?

If your organization is affiliated with a national body such as the American Hospital Association, the Family Service Association of America, or the National Council of Settlements and Community Centers, you may be able to get both technical assistance and written guidance from that body. Some years back, for example, the Child Welfare League of America published four guidebooks to help member agencies unscramble complexities of Title XX funding, cutting through the maze of federal and state guidelines.

Any of these organizations — local, state or national — can also guide you to local and state sources of funds, and may have materials available on the successful experiences of organizations similar to yours in other locales. Suggestions about useful sources of information on local, state, and federal funding are found at the end of this chapter.

EXERCISE 3.1
GETTING INFORMATION ON GOVERNMENT FUNDING SOURCES

(1) Look over Government Funding Source Inventory. Pick a federal, state, or local government agency that you want to become more familiar with. If it is a federal agency, you might wish to begin your information search by using the *Catalogue of Domestic Federal Assistance*. Some of the information may also be available from a colleague in your organization or in another organization with which you interact.

(2) Fill in the inventory with the information at hand. If there are blank spaces, where should you go for additional information? Will a telephone call or a letter yield that information? If so, be prepared to ask the specific question you want answered. Get the data and complete the form.

(3) Now do the same for funding sources from the other two levels of government.

Exercise 3.1
GOVERNMENT FUNDING SOURCE INVENTORY

1. **Level of Government**
   _____ Local
   _____ State
   _____ Federal
   _____ Other
   _____

11. **Funding Information**
    Assets $ _____
    Number of Awards available _____
    Average Award Size $ _____
    $ Range of Awards $_____ to
    $_____

12. Matching Fund Requirements
_____

2. Name of Agency _____
   _____

   Address _____   Can In-Kind Resources or In-
   _____   direct Costs Be Used? _____
                                        _____
   Telephone ( ) _____

                                      13. Kinds of Support Given
3. Contact Person _____   _____ Block Grants
                                          _____ Categorical Grants
   Title _____   _____ Formula Grants
                                          _____ Contracts
   Special Information _____   _____ Purchases of Service
   _____   _____ Other _____
                                          _____

4. Functional or Program Area in
   Which Awards Are Made   14. Uses Awards Can Be Put To
   _____   _____ Basic Research
   _____   _____ Assessment or Evaluation
   _____   _____ Programs and Services
                                          _____ Client Support
5. Geographic Areas _____   _____ Staffing
   _____   _____ Capital Expenditures
   _____   _____ Space/Equipment Rental
   _____   _____ Training and Trainee
                                                Support
6. Types of Organizations to   _____ Technical Assistance
   Which Awards Are Made _____   _____ Planning
   _____   _____ Coordination
   _____   _____ Demonstration or Start-up
7. Populations to Be Served by   _____ Ongoing Support
   Awards _____   Other _____
   _____   _____
   _____   _____
                                          _____
8. Current Priorities, If Any _____   _____
   _____
   _____   15. Materials Available
                                          _____ Application Kit
9. Restrictions, If Any _____   _____ Summaries of Previously
   _____   Funded Projects
   _____   _____ Guidelines
                                          _____ Sample Proposals
10. Funding Cycle _____   _____ Other _____
    _____   _____

16. Review Process Used _____
_____
_____
_____
_____

17. Due Dates for Proposals _____
_____
_____

Review Results Transmitted by
_____

18. Persons Currently or Recently
Involved in the Review Process
_____
_____
_____
_____
_____

19. Types of Assistance Available
_____ Written Materials
_____ Telephone Consultation
_____ Written Response to
Written Material
_____ In-Office Consultation
_____ On-Site Visits and Con-
sultation
_____ Other _____
_____
_____

20. Names of Decision Makers and
Program Persons Who Should
be Involved in Proposals to this
Source Including Client or
Community Representatives
_____
_____
_____
_____

21. Recent Awards in Area of
Interest
a. Award _____
Organization and Address
_____
_____
Contact Person _____
_____
_____

b. Award _____
Organization and Address
_____
_____

c. Award _____
Organization and Address
_____
_____

d. Award _____
Organization and Address
_____
_____
_____

22. Actions (to be) Taken
a. Phone Contacts _____
_____
b. Written Contacts _____
_____
c. Interviews or Meetings _____
_____
_____
d. Other _____
_____
_____

Inventory Compiled by   Date

BUILDING RELATIONSHIPS TO GOVERNMENT FUNDERS

As you complete Exercise 3.1 you will begin the process of building relationships with a funding organization and with one of the staff persons responsible for the allocations or technical assistance process. Remember, they are likely to be as interested in getting to know you as you are in finding out more about them. What kind of information are you ready to share? What can you say about

> the kind of organization you represent;
>
> its clients or members;
>
> the services it provides or is contemplating;
>
> the reasons you are seeking support;
>
> the amount you are seeking and for how long;
>
> the other sources you are also considering and the commitments made by those sources, if any;
>
> income from fees, fund raising events, and campaigns
>
> the nature of your staff;
>
> community involvement or support for your project;
>
> the needs or problems you intend to address.

If you are asked about any of these items on the telephone, can you give an answer succinctly, in one or two sentences? If you are asked to provide such information in a letter or preliminary outline, can you do it in two pages or less?

Part of the relationship-building process occurs through the exchange of information. Part of it occurs through the kinds of interpersonal relationships that are built up during that communication. The two persons quoted in the vignettes at the beginning of this chapter are clearly experienced in the grants and contracts processes. You may not have had as many experiences, and you may not be as clear as they are about what works and why. Look over the tow vignettes once again. This time read them carefully to uncover practice principles that can guide you in your search and in relationship building. A practice principle is just that, a *guide* to practice or to action.

For example, in the first illustration, you might paraphrase the first sentence in the form of a practice principle:

> Don't write a proposal unless you know in advance that you have a fighting chance of getting it funded.

How many more can you find?

EXERCISE 3.2
LISTING OF PRACTICE PRINCIPLES

(1) In simple declarative sentences, list all the practice principles you can find in the two vignettes, one beneath the other. Number them.

(2) Discuss them with colleagues and others who may have had considerable experience in the grantsmanship process or in working with government funding agencies. Ask them which of these are realistic or which they have found most useful.

(3) Based on their comments and on your own reactions, cross out those that you think are not adequate to guide you. Add others. And circle the numbers of those you think should guide you but which you may not yet feel comfortable in following. What must you do to increase your comfort or your capability?

SOME PERSONAL RECOLLECTIONS

I want to share a few experiences with you that may help add to your inventory of practice principles. In the late 1960s the National Institute of Mental Health (NIMH) determined that it would promote the development of continuing education (CE) activities among the mental health professions: social work, psychiatric nursing, psychiatry, and psychology. Announcements appeared in the *Federal Register* that grant funds would be available to professional schools, professional associations (for example, like the AMA and NASW), community mental health centers, and state mental health agencies. Subsequently, application information was mailed by the NIMH to deans and directors of those organizations. Sixty 3-year grants were awarded. The University of Michigan School of Social Work was one of the recipients.

A few years later, the school applied again to NIMH for another CE grant, this time to establish a mental health skills laboratory in the Detroit area. We were not funded. The original seed grant had been intended to help the school establish a capacity to do continuing education without continued federal support. From our perspective, the Detroit project was a new and different program. NIMH did not see it that way. Although Detroit-area agencies were in need we just did not have the capacity to extend our services to them without external support.

We were not the only interested parties, however. Although the original proposal had been rejected, we were in a good position to promote a new application. In the original project design, we had involved representatives of nineteen mental health agencies and of the Wayne County Community Mental Health Services Board. The original proposal was modified and resubmitted by the board, which also committed itself to an increasing share of financial responsibility. The lab was to be financially self-supporting at the end of three years. It was to be governed by a council to be made up of representatives from each of the participating mental health agencies. The school was to provide initial staffing, on contract, until the new lab was on its feet. There were no difficulties in getting the new project funded. Can you identify additional practice principles from the above? I will share another experience.

At about the same time as we were working on the lab, the Administration on Aging (AoA) was beginning to gear up for the establishment of Area Agencies on Aging throughout the United States. This was 1972. What turned out to be the 1973 Amendments to the Social Security Act — which included Title III, the basis on which area agencies were to be established — had not yet been passed by Congress. But the administration was confident that the bill would go through and wanted to be ready. You could not establish 600 or more regional planning agencies around the country without trained staff. AoA officials began looking around the country for universities that might be able to do the training once planners were hired. They looked first to universities that had both well-established institutes of gerontology and well-established schools of social work.

Michigan was such a place. One of our faculty members was also on one of AoA's advisory panels. He arranged to leave a book and a few articles on planning recently written by Michigan faculty with AoA staff. They got the hint. We were one of the universities solicited to submit a proposal. We were also one of the three to receive a grant. For the nest two years we worked closely with AoA staff on the design and implementation of the training program. As in any partnership, it was not always smooth sailing. The university staff saw itself fulfilling the obligations of a grant, with considerable flexibility in the way in which it should operate. AoA staff tended to view us as contractors, responsible for delivering a product at an agreed-upon time and for a predetermined cost. Despite some tension here and there, the partners completed the terms of the agreement and evaluated the relationship as being satisfactory. It was satisfactory primarily because the consumers of the training program, newly appointed area planners, found what they had learned to be directly applicable to their work.

In contrast to these examples, in 1982 I submitted a proposal to train public welfare officials in grantsmanship and in work with the private sector. Federal guidelines were published by the Office of Human

Development in the *Federal Register*. The funds to be allocated had been collected from previously established categorical funding programs, and were to be awarded on a competitive and discretionary basis. The amounts available were not large; the deadline only six or seven weeks from the time of publication of the guidelines. The review criteria were not clearly described.

Nevertheless, because money was tight, about 8,000 applications were submitted. Fewer than 10 percent were funded. No one received any technical assistance. It was not even possible to find out who was responsible for providing information on specific programs for which funding was announced. I should have known better than to apply. A colleague in another state who did receive an award later complained to me, "It's been a nightmare all along. The feds want to know everything we are doing but they don't have the staff to monitor events properly or even to understand what is going on. Never saw a disarray like this in my life."

In the AoA and NIMH examples, federal agencies had clear ideas of what they wanted accomplished and were ready to invest in technical assistance and other supports in order to increase the likelihood of grantee success. In the last example, the government's intent was not clear, nor was it properly staffed to achieve whatever its objectives may have been.

Similar situations often prevail, for at least a limited time, during administrative changeovers, particularly when the new administration — at the federal, state, or local levels — has different priorities from a previous administration. They are also likely to occur when responsibility is shifted from one agency to another or from one level of government to another. The states, for example, strongly resisted efforts by the Reagan administration to shift responsibility from the federal to the state levels for the funding of what had been categorical programs through newly envisioned block grant mechanisms. The state agencies just did not have the staffing capacities to both allocate funds and provide adequate technical assistance.

Despite the difficulties that changes in accustomed ways of doing business may present, they also provide new opportunities. Disarray or confusion in a funding agency may provide you and your organization with an opportunity to share information on local needs or on the severity of a problem that should be addressed. You might do so at a public hearing, through reports sent to government officials, perhaps indirectly through a state senator, a city council member, or their staffs. This can be your opportunity to shape the direction of future funding patterns.

How well are you positioned to take advantage of an opportunity when it presents itself, or to turn a predicament into an opportunity?

REVIEW

Both funders and recipients of funding awards have a stake in each other. Funders are often on the lookout for organizations or individuals that can perform the work they have been entrusted to support. Petitioners can reduce their dependency on funders if (1) alternative sources of supply are available; (2) they can indicate a capacity to do what the funder needs done; and (3) they can provide the funder with access to other needed resources: populations, legitimacy, and so on. This is especially true of government funding agencies that are required by public mandate to provide assistance in areas of social and economic development.

The most comprehensive source of information on federal programs is the *Catalogue of Federal Domestic Assistance*. It is a good starting point in your search for the appropriate agency or funding program. Some states also publish similar catalogues. You may have to search out listings by program or population served from various state agencies. If there is a state office for the League for the Human Services, you might get leads there. Other places to get information are professional associations, the staff of coordinating councils and planning agencies, colleagues in other agencies, and so on. There are also a number of advocacy groups, search services and consulting firms available to help.

Most government funding organizations provide applicants with written guidelines and/or application forms. Some provide extensive technical assistance and consultation in the program development and proposal writing stages of the process. Some continue to provide technical assistance along with their monitoring activities after a project has been funded. The more established the funding source, the closer it is to your organization geographically and functionally, the more personal and extensive the services are that your organization may expect.

SUGGESTIONS FOR FURTHER READING

Start with these government sources.

Catalogue of Federal Domestic Assistance

Published annually in May, the *Catalogue* has semi-annual (Fall) and sometimes quarterly supplements. The most comprehensive source of information on federal granting programs, it describes agencies, funding programs, sums available, where to get additional application information, and so on. It is functionally indexed by agency, program name, subject matter, popular designation, and eligible grantee. The *Catalogue* can be purchased from the Government Printing Office, but you may be able to get it free through your congressional representative's office. You will also find it in most public libraries.

United States Government Manual

Published each year, included (as up-to-date as possible) names, addresses, and phone numbers of key government granting agencies. Sources as above. Order from Government Printing Office.

Federal Register

A daily publication that contains detailed information on proposed rules, guidelines, and other important financial information on specific grant programs. The *Register* tells when grant monies are to become available, amounts to be spent. It provides current information on new programs that may not be in the *Catalogue.* Most major libraries subscribe. Order from Government Printing Office.

Commerce Business Daily

The is the federal government's shopping list and want ad that announces contract opportunities and grants over $25,000. Even if you do not contract with the government directly, you might be able to subcontract with an organization or company that does. Order from Government Printing Office. Check current prices.

Agency Publications

Do not stop there. Use the above to get on the mailing lists of all appropriate funding agencies in your field. Get the news before it happens! No sense in hearing about an award after it has been made. Get on the mailing lists of the relevant federal, state, and local agencies.

You may also be able to get useful information from a number of newsletters and magazines.

Capitol Publications, Inc., Suite G-12, 2430 Pennsylvania Avenue, Washington , DC 20037, publishes the following newsletters weekly, except the last week in December.

Health Grants and Contracts Weekly
Federal Grants and Contracts Weekly: Selected Project Opportunities for the Educational Community

Morris Associates, Inc., at 1346 Connecticut Avenue, NW, Washington, DC 20036, publishes

The MH-MR Report (semi-monthly)
Health Systems Report (weekly)

Find out about other sources in your area of interest. Check with your professional association, another agency, a national organization you may be affiliated with.

Several books may also be useful to you:

DesMarais, Philip. *How to Get Government Grants.* New York: Public Service Materials Center, 1977.

Stephen Nowland et al. (eds.), *How to Get Money for the Arts and Humanities, Drugs, Alcohol, Human Services, and Health.* Radnor, PA: Human Resources Network, Chillon Book Co., 1975.

Other materials from the Human Resources Network:

How to Get Money for Conservation and Community Development, 1975

How to get Money for Youth, the Elderly, the Handicapped, Women, and Civil Liberties, 1975

How about other state and local sources of information? Check with your state League of the Human Services or with the staff of a state legislator who is actively involved in promoting legislation or overseeing programs in your area of concern — child welfare, protective services for the elderly, health care, and so on. Go directly to the agency that is responsible for those services. Contact the appropriate official and ask about contract or grant programs for organizations like yours. You may have to go through a few different offices before you reach the right person. But do not be discouraged. They may not know how to find you either. Get whatever literature they provide. Ask for summaries of recent grants or contracts awarded.

The materials you are seeking might be located with a semi-independent contractor. For example, the state Department of Labor may contract out with a private firm for all of its training activities, and this firm may subcontract out on a competitive basis to organizations like your own. A city council may allocate its funds for neighborhood development and other services indirectly through a community development corporation (CDC). If that is the case the CDC is the address for information on available funds.

Chapter 4

BUILDING ON A STRONG FOUNDATION
Seeking Foundation Grants

VIGNETTE 6: A REJECTION SPURS A NEW PROGRAM ON

We started out as an offshoot of the Women's Crisis Center. The center is mostly volunteer run: women raising each other's consciousness, helping each other when the going gets rough. For some women it's really rough. Three years ago, when the economy went sour, we noticed an increase in calls from women who were complaining of all kinds of abusive treatment at home. Some desperately needed to get away. None of the other services in town could provide them with even temporary shelter. We were able to help some by putting them up in private homes or in hotels, and the Y took a few. This cost a lot and it just wasn't safe.

What we needed was a safe house. But the federal government had just cut its program subsidies to spouse abuse shelters so it didn't look like we were going to be able to get government dollars. The Weelington Foundation had a reputation for concerns about child abuse and also for supporting family development activities. It seemed like a natural.

It didn't take long to write up a proposal. One of our board members had located a piece of property that we thought was sufficiently isolated to provide safety. And we got all sorts of advice from other safe houses around the state on how to staff and manage the facility. We thought we had a pretty good proposal. And one of the foundation staff members encouraged us to submit. "If it strengthens families, we're interested," Frank Santier of the foundation told me. "Send it in."

We did. We got turned down. I was stunned. I called Mr. Santier and asked the reason. "There are two," he explained. "One is substantive, the other is a matter of form." On the substantive matter, he continued, we had emphasized the needs of the women for safety and had described services aimed at providing them with greater independence. Many of them, our proposal emphasized, needed to get away from their husbands at least temporarily, if not permanently. "The foundation," he told me, "is interested in promoting family stability and development; not family dissolution. The husband is the villain in your proposal and the wife, the victim. We see them both as victims."

That really got me thinking. Were we so militant as women that we had forgotten that a marriage is made up of two persons? If we followed the Weelington Foundation's logic, would we have to redesign our program, offer services to men? Wouldn't they resist services, especially if offered by a Women's Crisis Center? Should we consider some kind of court-ordered program? But wouldn't that mean we would have to get women to press charges and wouldn't that be defeating in terms of family stability?

We needed some help on this if we were to go back to the foundation. Some of my colleagues and some of our board members didn't want anything to do with the foundation. They thought we could go our own way and find funding elsewhere. I wasn't so sure. I thought the foundation was on to something with its criticism. I decided to visit the foundation office and explore our interests with them some more.

I brought along Marci Maslow, a staffer on the Child Guidance Clinic that had received funds from the foundation in previous years. Marci is one of our active volunteers. She came in part to give me moral support, in part to give me legitimacy, in part to give me some ideas.

I was really surprised. Frank Santier and Rosabeth Mitchel of the foundation staff gave us a full hour and a half. In that discussion we explored all kinds of possibilities to complement the safe house project: men's discussion groups, referral of spouses to the community mental health center and to the family and children's agency, employment counseling. Problem was, the project was getting too big for us to handle. "We'll have to see what part of all this we can carve out for ourselves," I concluded the meeting and thanked them both for their time.

We did submit a new proposal. And we did get partial funding. The rest was raised through a capital drive and through an expanded allocation from the United Way; several of the other United Way agencies vouched for us and for the need to set up a shelter.

Oh, yes. The matter of form. Our original proposal had been 38 pages long. It was loaded with details on the facility and how we would manage it, on the documentation of the problem, and so on. The second proposal was only 8 pages long. It had very few details, but it did spell out how we were going to contribute to family stability and development. And it did spell out our capability of doing the job in collaboration with other local human service agencies. The reviewers were satisfied; they didn't want to be bothered by details.

As Rosabeth Mitchel told me before we resubmitted, "Staff at the foundation may be interested in lots of details, and if you get funding we'll want regular reports. But our lay people are the ones who make decisions. They are busy people. We can't expect them to read a proposal if it's more than five to eight pages in length. They don't want details. They trust us to get them. They want to deal with policy issues. Don't overwhelm them with more than they need."

VIGNETTE 7: WHY JUST A POSTCARD?

I've always been interested in neighborhoods and in empowerment. A few years ago a federal grant for neighborhood involvement might have been a real possibility. Today, it's out of the cards, especially for the kinds of purposes I was interested in. So I figured our best bet was to look for foundation support.

I started my search by going to the community library. It happens that we have one of the Foundation Center's "cooperating collections," here so I felt pretty sure we could get the information we needed. The search began with a review of the last couple of years' issues of the Foundations Grants Index. The index comes out once a year and it refers to descriptions of grants in the amounts of $5000 or more made by about 500 foundations. Whenever I found something that fit, I checked out the more detailed description of the grant in one of the issues of the Foundation Center News, a journal that comes out six times or so each year.

Well, I got a few good prospects. But it wasn't enough. So I decided to invest a little more time and a few bucks. The Foundation Center started a printout service a couple of years back called COMSEARCH. It prints out names of foundations and projects in a whole gamut of different subjects.

I found several categories of printout subjects that seemed to fit our interests: films, documents and audiovisuals (we were thinking of involving residents in videotaping the community); mental health; public health; orchestras and musical performances; the aged; the handicapped; Blacks, Hispanics; environmental protection; crime and law; civil rights; and community and urban development. These are the subjects of printouts published each year, so you can't tailor a printout to your own specs. Still, by looking each one over, I was able to spot a number of foundations that dealt with several topics of interest to us.

Having located 67 likely prospects, I sent them each a two-page letter describing briefly what we intended to do and asking whether or not the foundation might be interested. The letter, I might add, was textbook perfect. It even included a Xerox of a photograph of one of our neighborhoods as an eye-catcher.

I got 65 responses, most of them on mimeographed postcards; all of them turndowns. No explanation, no nothin'! Why just a postcard?

FOUNDATIONS HAVE AGENDAS

The message in both vignettes is clear: foundations have agendas, and they are not about to provide funding to groups, individuals, or organizations whose requests do not complement those objectives. Before you decide to modify your agenda significantly, however, you should know something about foundations and about what they fund.

In 1983 foundations allocated somewhat less than $3 billion to nonprofit organizations and charitable causes. That is no small amount; but proportionately, it is not all that much either. Of the $60+ billion in nongovernmental allocations to nonprofit organizations, over 80 percent came from individuals, almost 10 percent through bequests, about 5 percent from corporations, and (as the $3 billion figure implies) less than 5 percent from foundations. The contributions of foundations to what is generally called the voluntary sector, though substantial, are not necessarily decisive. Moreover, these contributions are spread out among a number of subcategories of the voluntary sector: education and research (e.g., colleges, school-related activities, research and development); culture (fine arts, performances, museums and historic preservations, libraries, broadcasting); religion (churches and religious publications); health services (hospitals, nursing homes, preventive and public health activities); community development (conservation, environmental protection, public education, social action), *and* human services (including financial assistance, legal aid, special programs for youth, the aged, families and so on).

According to the authors of the *1982 Foundation Grants Index,* 369 of the nearly 19,000 bona fide private foundations studied gave 45 percent of the grants awarded in the previous year. (There may be as many as 30,000 to 40,000 private foundations in America.) About one-fourth of those foundations accounted for half of the number of grants and 77 percent of the funds allocated. *Education* and *health* have, in recent years, each accounted for 20 to 25 percent of the money allocated, and *human service agencies* for about 16 percent. This has changed dramatically since 1981. Today the human services receive one out of every three or four dollars allocated by foundations. The reasons for the change are not hard to find. The recession in the early 1980s, with its high unemployment rate and the substantial cutbacks in federal funding for social services that accompanied it, put enormous pressures on foundations to respond to human needs at the local level. Research-related activities were cut back, as was support to hospitals and other health providers on the assumption that Medicare and Medicaid funds would substitute. In addition to increased funding for human services, contributions to community cultural activities also reflected a rise from about 14 percent of the allocations to over 17 percent. In both cases, grant funds were clearly earmarked for local giving.

Although this may be a hopeful sign to some local agencies, foundation dollars are limited and will never be able to make up, in any substantial way, for recent cuts in public programs. Moreover, increased demand on their resources and aggressiveness on the part of local applicants has forced many foundations to reevaluate their policies and funding strategies. "It's taking us longer than we thought," explained a foundation officer to me, "but we have just got to complete our reassessment if we are going to be fair to those who may wish to apply." Different types of foundations have different interests. And within each category of foundation, interest and priorities are likely to differ further.

The term "foundation" tends to be used somewhat loosely. Because it connotes a certain amount of prestige, its use has been adopted by fund-raising groups, organizations that provide direct services, pressure groups, and not a few outright rackets. The term "private foundation." on the other hand, came to have a very specific connotation. *Private foundations.* according to the 1969 Tax Reform Act, must have charitable, religious, educational, scientific, or cultural purposes.

TYPES OF PHILANTHROPIC FOUNDATIONS

There are a number of different types of foundations, each with their own characteristics. Many general-purpose philanthropic foundations are identified as *private foundations.* These have broad charters and often rather large endowments. The large ones operate independently and are professionally staffed. Many private foundations will support only pioneering or innovative programs and will be reluctant to support projects or organizations for long periods of time. Although in times of emergency some have been known to bail out a supplicant, they are more apt to see themselves as responsible for providing seed money to launch new programs that will in time become self-supporting. Some of the largest — the Ford Foundation, for example — also concern themselves with initiating social experiments that are likely to have an impact on public policy and ultimately on public expenditures. Other large foundations include the Robert Wood Johnson, Rockefeller, Kellogg, and Carnegie foundations. Medium-sized foundations include the Mott and Edna McConnel Clark foundations. Although no longer connected to industry, many of their initial donors were large industrialists. Thus, the Clark Foundation's portfolio began with large bequest of funds from Avon Products, and the Mott Foundation built its portfolio around a donation of General Motors stock.

These foundations, however, operate fully autonomously, *independent* from the businesses and even the individuals who founded them. They have their own boards of directors that make the final decisions on any grants to be made, and for this reason they are often referred to as *independent* foundations. The key people in the grants process are the staff members responsible for given areas of concern (e.g., child welfare, job training, community education).

These staff members are the ones with whom you will have contact, and they will screen proposals before any are to be submitted to the board. They also recommend whether or not a grant is to be made and the size of the award. Although some of the staff members tend to be national or even international in the scope of their interests, others will be both knowledgeable about and responsible for the foundation's involvement in the local community or with such functional concerns as aging or youth. A number of foundations that had previously identified themselves as general-purpose foundations have through their reevaluation processes become special-purpose foundations.

In contrast, *community foundations* are set up exclusively to serve a specific geographic area, usually a city, and its sometimes adjacent townships. Cleveland established the first community foundation in the years immediately preceding World War II. There are now more than 300 others throughout the United States. Today they account for about 3 percent of all foundation assets and allocations in the United States. Initially established to ensure proper stewardship of trusts and bequests, community foundations now actively seek funds from individual and corporate donors who prefer to have their philanthropic responsibilities administered by professional foundation managers. Several report allocations from local government sources as well.

Community foundations are concerned primarily with local needs. At one time they tended only to sponsor such cultural programs as the local philharmonic or a summer "concert in the park" series. Today they are increasingly involved in human service and community development activities. These include downtown reconstruction, the building of pocket parks, and the support of social services for which other funds may not be readily available. Community foundations frequently seek to use their funds as venture capital to attract other grants, possibly from government or industrial sources.

Community foundations' trustees include prominent citizens who make all final decisions. Some make genuine efforts to represent all segments of the population. However, as with independent foundations, staff are often gatekeepers and the primary decision makers. Although many trustees and staff may be savvy about local needs, they may also need to be educated. Your success as a fund raiser will be much improved if the staff are knowledgeable about your agency's services and the needs of the populations you are concerned about. It may take a while before you can properly position your organization to make an application. Media and public awareness campaigns may increase your chances considerably.

Family foundations make up by far the largest numbers of private foundations in the United States. They vary greatly in size and areas of interest. Their endowments are generally under $5 million, and many may be only in the $10,000 to $200,000 range. Although some have boards, the preferences of family members who make major contributions generally prevail. Few have professional staffs; some family foundations are administered by a trustee who is probably a private attorney, a local banker, or a trust corporation with many other responsibilities.

Some family foundations are clearly tax shelters. The goal may be to provide university scholarships to worthy students, but recipients may be limited to friends and relatives of the family. Many have religious purposes. Some are connected with social agencies, the primary supporter of an endowment program for specific projects in those organizations. Family foundations are sometimes on the lookout for good prospects — people and organizations to fund. Once on a family foundation's list, you may remain on it indefinitely. But getting on that list is another matter. It may require knowing someone in the family or knowing someone who knows someone. Because most do not have professional staff, they may not know how to deal with most unsolicited proposals; some will not even acknowledge receipt of your inquiry.

Recent concern with corporate America's social responsibilities has focused attention on *company (sponsored) foundations.* You are probably aware that corporations are permitted to make charitable contributions of up to 10 percent of their pretax earnings, and frequently they establish foundations to administer those funds. As with the others, company foundations are tax exempt and nonprofit entities. Although separate from their parent companies, their boards tend to consist almost exclusively of company officers. Examples include the Alcoa Foundation, the Sears Roebuck Foundation, the Exxon Education Fund, and the Aetna Foundation. You will not only recognize the company names, but may be aware of some educational or cultural programs sponsored by these foundations.

About 5 percent of the assets owned by American foundations fall into this category. Today most of the funds allocated tend to be confined to communities where the parent company has its officers or plants. In general, grants are made for the support of institutions or agencies that benefit the company's employees, its stock holders, or others with whom it has business relationships. Some corporations have used foundations to enhance their public images through the sponsorship of cultural and other programs. We will come back to this concern in the next chapter.

In some communities, corporation executives have banded together to increase the size of their giving programs. The Ford Foundation, in fact, has encouraged corporations in cities throughout the United States to increase their giving by offering matching funds that deal exclusively with economic development at the grass roots level. In San Francisco, several executives have organized a "2% Club" that is actively involved in inducing corporations to contribute more to the local community.

All of these foundations can be categorized as *nonoperating;* that is, they fund programs that other organizations take operational responsibility for. In contrast, there are a growing number of *operating foundations* that solicit funds for their own purposes, and give those funds to pet projects and programs they themselves sponsor or operate. Examples include universities that set up foundations to raise money and reallocate to university building or scholarship funds, homes for the aged, local philharmonics, museums, and the like. It is unlikely that these foundations would be receptive to your organization's interests unless they clearly further those of the foundation.

FINDING OUT ABOUT FOUNDATIONS

While there is a great deal of information about foundations in general, you will find that it can be somewhat difficult to get the specific information you may need. The larger foundations will tend to have annual reports, special project summaries, and even information packets aimed at encouraging eligible applications. Most foundations, however, are either unstaffed or understaffed. And unlike government bureaus, they are not required by law to establish clear guidelines and criteria or to provide technical assistance. You may consider yourself lucky even to get a mimeographed "thanks for your inquiry" postcard from some. While IRS regulations have opened their books to public scrutiny, foundations are not required to make it easy for you to scrutinize them. Making themselves inaccessible or unresponsive is one way of reducing the demand for their generally limited funds.

There are, fortunately, a number of general references and a wide variety of periodicals as well as some search services available to you. A good place to start is by examining the materials developed by the Foundation Center. Another is by examining your own state foundation directory. A third is by subscribing to appropriate journals, special interest associations, and to commercial search services. None of these may be as useful as information you might get from a colleague or a friend who has had the good fortune of being funded by a foundation. But be careful: word-of-mouth information can be unreliable. Foundations change priorities; they often are faced with eligible requests for funds that total ten or more times the sums available.

The Foundation Funding Source Inventory can help you in your efforts to get accurate and up-to-date information on foundations you are interested in.

EXERCISE 4.1
GETTING INFORMATION ON FOUNDATION
FUNDING SOURCES

(1) Look over the Foundation Funding Source Inventory. Pick a foundation that you want to become more familiar with. If you are not sure where to start, try the resources available from a nearby Foundation Center Cooperating Library, or get the information from one of the four Foundation Center Offices (New York, San Francisco, Washington, D.C., or Cleveland). For the address of the nearest Cooperating Collection (Library), call (800) 424-9836.

(2) Fill in the inventory with the information you have collected. If there are too many blank spaces, contact the foundation directly, or use an available search service.

Exercise 4.1
FOUNDATION FUNDING SOURCE INVENTORY

1. Type of Foundation
   _____ Independent, General Purpose
   _____ Independent, Special Purpose
   _____ Community
   _____ Family
   _____ Company
   _____ Operational

2. Name of Foundation _____
   Address _____
   _____
   Telephone ( ) _____

3. Contact Person _____
   Title _____
   _____
   Special Information _____
   _____
   _____
   _____

4. Functional or Program Areas in Which Awards Are Made _____
   _____
   _____
   _____

11. Funding Information
    Assets $ _____
    _____
    Number of Awards Available
    _____
    Average Award Size $ _____
    $ Range of Awards $ _____
    to $ _____

12. Matching Fund Requirements
    _____
    Can In-Kind Resources or Indirect Costs Be Use? _____
    _____

13. Uses Awards Can Be Put To
    _____ Basic Research
    _____ Assessment or Evaluation
    _____ Programs and Services
    _____ Client Support
    _____ Staffing
    _____ Capital Expenditures
    _____ Space/Equipment Rental
    _____ Training and Trainee Support

5. Geographic Preferences or Restrictions _____
_____
_____

6. Types of Organizations to Which Awards Are Made _____
_____
_____

7. Special Characteristics of Populations the Foundation Is Most Interested In (ethnic, economic status, religion)
_____
_____
_____

8. Current Priorities, Special Interests _____
_____
_____
_____

9. Restrictions, If Any _____
_____
_____

10. Funding Cycle _____

____ Technical Assistance
____ Planning
____ Coordination
____ Demonstration or Start-up
____ Ongoing Support
Other _____
_____
_____

14. Materials Available _____
____ Application Kit
____ Summaries of Previously Funded Projects
____ Guidelines
____ Sample Proposals
____ Other _____
_____

15. Names of Other Foundations with Similar Scope or Interest _____
_____
_____
_____
_____

16. Review Process Used _____
_____
_____
_____
_____

17. Due Dates for Proposals _____
_____

Review Results Transmitted by
_____

18. Persons Currently or Recently Involved in the Review Process
_____
_____
_____
_____
_____

21. Recent Awards in Area of Interest
a. Award _____
Organization and Address
_____
_____

Contact Person _____
_____

b. Award _____
Organization and Address
_____
_____

c. Award _____
Organization and Address
_____

19. Types of Assistance Available
    _____ Written Materials
    _____ Telephone Consultation
    _____ Written Response to
          Written Material
    _____ In-Office Consultation
    _____ On-Site Visits and Con-
          sultation
    _____ Other _____

20. Names of Decision Makers and
    Program Persons Who Should
    Be Involved in Proposals to this
    Source Including Client or
    Community Representatives

    d. Award _____
       Organization and Address

22. Actions (to be) Taken
    a. Phone Contacts _____

    b. Written Contacts _____

    c. Interviews or Meetings _____

    d. Other _____

Inventory Compiled by   Date

THE FOUNDATION CENTER AND
THE RESOURCES IT HAS AVAILABLE

Because information on foundations was so difficult to come by, the Foundation Center was established in 1956. Its offices were located in New York, where many of the largest foundations were located. Its support currently comes from some 100 or so large and small foundations throughout the United States. The center helps grantseekers to sort among nearly 20,000 active foundations for those which might be most interested in their projects. Foundations support the center because they, too, want grantseekers to avoid taking a hit-or-miss approach. A more targeted search process relieves foundations of the need to distribute basic information to everyone who requests it.

The center publishes reference books on foundations and disseminates information through a nationwide public information and education program in the interest of matching foundation interests with nonprofit organization needs. It will not direct you to particular foundations, no will it arrange introductions, but it will provide you free access to its information at its New York office or at any one of its three branches (Cleveland, San Francisco, or Washington, D.C.), and through its 105 Cooperating (Library) Collections. These are located throughout the United States, often in university, community college, or public libraries, or in the offices of supporting foundations. To find out where the nearest collection is, call toll free (800) 424-9836. You will find that the reference librarian will be more than helpful in guiding you to the appropriate sources. Collections include Foundation Center materials and scores of other books, articles, and periodicals.

The center publishes five general directories and the *Foundation Grants Index Annual,* plus a number of COMSEARCH printouts. You were given some idea of what these services can do for you from the second vignette at the start of this chapter. I will share some additional information about these sources of information with you, and my guess about why the grantseeker quoted received only "thanks but no thanks" postcard replies.

Let us start with the directories. The single best source on corporate, independent, and community foundations is the *Foundations Directory,* now in its ninth edition. New volumes come out every few years. In the latest edition you will find information on between 3000 and 4000 foundations, including those that give grants that total $100,000 or more each year and whose assets exceed a million dollars. These are the sources of almost 90 percent of all grant dollars allocated by foundations. The directory is organized by state with foundations listed alphabetically. It is also cross-indexed so that you can locate the foundations that are the likeliest prospects for your grant application. Information on assets, numbers of awards and size of awards, key officials, and, in fact, on much of what is included on the inventory in Exercise 4.1, will be found here. But the information is skimpy.

You may also want to examine two other directories: *Source Book Profiles* and *Corporation Foundation Profiles.* The 1982 edition of the *Source Book Profiles* included three- to six-page entries on the 1000 largest foundations, including 200 company and 25 community foundations, breaking down each one's giving by subject area, type of grant, and type of recipient. The *Corporate Foundation Profiles* includes similar data on the company foundations, plus financial data on 300 or so additional corporate foundations. Fifty or so of the corporate profiles are updated each year.

Two other directories may be of interest to you. The *National Data Book* includes virtually all of the currently active grantmaking foundations. Foundation entries include name, address, financial officer, and fiscal data — and an indication of whether or not a particular foundation issues an annual report. Included are all foundations that give more than one dollar per year in grants; for example, 87 percent gave under $100,000 per year. Some of these are the small foundations in your community or state that might be likely prospects for a small award.

The *Foundation Grants to Individuals* directory zeros in on the 950 or so foundations that cumulatively give almost one hundred million dollars in grants and awards to individuals each year. Over 44,000 people receive grants from these foundations for educational assistance, study abroad, research, or special projects in the arts, sciences, and humanities. You have probably heard of the Guggenheim Foundation. How many more are you aware of?

Before we turn to the *Foundation Grants Index,* a word about the *Foundation Center News.* The *News* is a professional journal of interest to all those in the philanthropy business, published by the Council on Foundations on a bimonthly basis. It can be ordered from the Council at 1828 L Street, N.W., Washington, D.C. 20036. Foundation officers read it to find out what is going on and to chart trends in giving. You might find it useful for the same purposes. About half the pages in each issue describe grants (reported to the center) that were made within the last month or two in amounts of $5000 or more to nonprofit organizations. The *Index* comes out each year and helps you locate the appropriate description of the more than 22,000 grants described in the *News.* The *Index* cross-references grants by foundation, by geographic area, by interest or subject matter. It is the quickest way to locate information on foundations that made grants in areas of interest to you during the previous year.

If your head is reeling from an information overload, let me suggest another way of cutting through the enormous amounts of information available through the center. Try locating the appropriate COM-SEARCH printouts. *Geographic Printouts* list and describe actual grants made to organizations in two cities (Washington and New York), eleven states (California, Illinois, Massachusetts, Michigan, Minnesota, New Jersey, New York, North Carolina, Ohio, Pennsylvania, and Texas), and four regions (the Northeast — Maine, New Hampshire, Rhode Island, Vermont, Connecticutt; the Southeast — Florida, Georgia, Alabama, Mississippi, Louisiana, South Carolina; the Northwest — Washington and Oregon; and the Rocky Mountains — Arizona, New Mexico, Colorado, Utah, Nevada, Idaho, Montana, and Wyoming).

Special Topics Printouts list the 1000 largest foundations in the United States by asset size and by annual grant award totals; the 600 largest company-sponsored foundations; and the 1450 operating foundations that administer their own projects or programs. There is also a new series of COMSEARCH printouts, *Broad Topics,* covering grants for (1) arts and cultural programs, (2) business and employment, (3) children and youth, (4) higher education, (5) hospitals and medical care, (6) museums, (7) science programs, (8) social science programs, (9) women and girls, (10) international and foreign programs; and (11) minorities.

Probably the most targeted information is to be found in the new series *Subject Printouts.* You can obtain a complete list from the Foundation Center. These are organized under topic headings such as communication, education, health, and cultural activities. Under a particular heading — welfare for example — there are subtopics: housing, civil rights, and community development. Unfortunately you cannot just punch in a few key variables into a Foundation Center computer in order to get a personalized printout tailored to your specific concerns. But the standardized COMSEARCH printouts will certainly help you identify the likeliest prospects. Why, then, did this approach not work out for the author of the second vignette?

See notes / run off —

A MORE PERSONALIZED APPROACH

It has been my experience that buckshot approaches rarely work. Photocopied, "to whom it may concern"-type letters are likely to get mimeographed or photocopied responses. I have found that it often pays to place a call first, ask the receptionist for the appropriate project staffer or other person to talk to, and then to talk to that person — much as I recommended you talk to government officials. Foundation personnel are not as obligated as government to give you time, nor will they necessarily refer you to another, more appropriate funding source. However, if you are on target, you will know right away. Your letter can then be addressed to a specific person. It can be tailored to the kinds of initial feedback that person gave you, and it can refer to the foundation's current interests and priorities — those that complement the focus of the project you will be proposing.

Remember that many foundations, especially the smaller ones, have no paid staff. They may be managed by a part-time volunteer, often a member of the family that has put up the money, and so will find it difficult to respond to your inquiries. Although well-staffed, the larger foundations may be so inundated with requests that they will respond only to certain types of inquiries. I have found that many foundations do not consider fully fleshed-out proposals without prior contact. Nor will they respond to long and detailed inquiries. You might find the following tips helpful. They come from my own experiences, but if yours are different, follow your own instincts.

TIP 1. When approaching a foundation cold, use the telephone first and then keep your correspondence brief. Your cover letter should be no longer than a single page. It should include information on who you are, why you feel your project is important to your organization, and why you think it might be of interest to the foundation. Attach a one- or two-page description of the project for which you would like funding. You might prefer including two or three descriptions as bait. This will give you some idea of what the foundation is biting on this year. But don't allow the total number of pages to exceed two or three.

TIP 2. In your one- or two-page proposal outline, specify the objectives you are trying to reach, how you want to reach them, and how long it will take to get to where you want to go. Point out the significance of the project for those persons being served as well as for others who may want to replicate the project elsewhere. Indicate how much the project might cost. And mention something about the accountability or evaluative procedures you'll be using. Pitch to the specific interests of the foundation. If you know a foundation is interested in health *research,* for example, don't submit a *training* proposal for physicians and nurses.

TIP 3. If at all possible, avoid going in cold. The smaller foundations especially like to deal with people or organizations they know. If they publish annual reports, these should tell you who has been funded in recent years. Check with someone else who has received a grant from the foundation. Get a sense of what the foundation's real priorities are. And if possible, get an introduction to a foundation board member or to the foundation's executive officer or grants manager through someone else who has already had a successful experience with the foundation.

You will have additional ideas of your own or may have gathered them from colleagues who have had experience in dealing with foundations. Develop a set of tips or practice principles to guide you in your search and in your relationships to foundations. Use Exercise 4.2 as a guide.

EXERCISE 4.2
LISTING OF PRACTICE PRINCIPLES

(1) Review the practice principles you identified for working with government funding sources. Which of these apply to foundations? Which would have to be modified or eliminated?

(2) Identify additional practice principles in this chapter and add those from your experience or the experiences of colleagues.

(3) Draw up a new list of practice principles appropriate to work with foundations, or add to and modify the list you designed for government sources, indicating (a) which are universal, (b) which apply only to public sources, and (c) which apply to foundation sources.

REVIEW

There are more than 30,000 philanthropic foundations in the United States. Of these, over 20,000 provide grants and other funding to nonprofit organizations. A relatively small number — about 100 of the largest foundations — account for roughly one-fourth of the funds awarded. There are several kinds of philanthropic foundations. The vast majority, about 19,000, are generally defined as private, general purpose, or specific interest foundations. Although many have national or international agendas, most orient their funding activities to local communities or to specific types of organizations. Such *independent foundations* as Ford or Mellon are among the best known. *Community foundations* are a growing phenomenon; these are exclusively local in their orientations. They allocate funds generated from bequests, corporate donors, individual benefactors, and even local government allocations.

Company (sponsored) foundations are perhaps the fastest growing category in terms of assets and funds allocated. Their assets currently account for approximately 5 percent of all foundation assets. Awards tend to be made in ways that complement the sponsoring company's interests, serve the employees of the company, or deal with issues in communities in which the company has plants or headquarters. *Family foundations,* often identifying themselves as private foundations, tend, in fact, to be exceedingly private. They are generally very limited in their focuses, even if official statements would suggest broad interests or general purposes. Many aim at support of religious or ethnic causes, organizations or individuals with appropriate backgrounds and characteristics. *Operating foundations* are of a different order. Although some are fully funded, many engage in fund-raising activities. Grants are allocated to programs and projects administered by the foundation itself.

The Foundation Center was established almost thirty years ago for the express purpose of making information on foundations more accessible to grantseekers, to the academic community, and to the general public. Its headquarters are in New York and it has three regional branch offices. In addition, it supports a growing network of cooperating collections: reference materials generally located in public libraries or in university, community college, and foundation office libraries throughout the United States. Many of these resources are published by the center itself. These include a journal, five directories, computer printouts, and an index.

Foundations tend to have very limited and highly targeted agendas. Unfortunately, many do not publicize their efforts, and specific information or guidelines may be hard to come by. Proposals that do not articulate directly with a foundation's concerns, or that arrive unsolicited and unannounced, may go unheeded. This poses a special challenge to the grantseeker to get accurate, up-to-date information, and to put his or her organization in position to be sought after and welcomed by appropriate foundations.

SUGGESTIONS FOR FURTHER READING

Start with publications of the Foundation Center. These can be found at one of the 105 or more Cooperating Collections, at one of the Center's four offices, or can be ordered directly from the Center at 888 Seventh Avenue, New York, NY 10106.

The Foundation Directory (9th ed.)
Source Book Profiles
The National Data Book
Corporate Foundation Profiles
Foundation Grants to Individuals
The Foundation Grants Index Annual Volume
plus COMSEARCH printouts by *Subject Matter, Geographic Area, Broad Topics*

In addition, you can order the following publications from the Foundation Center.

Kurzig, Carol. *Foundation Fundamentals: A Guide for Grantseekers* 1981.
Includes information on what foundations are and how they work, how they fit into the total funding pattern for nonprofits, who gets grants, and how to find a foundation with an interest in your field. It also includes a proposal research checklist and suggestions on how to present your ideas.

1982 Foundations Today, April 1982.
A 24-page state-of-the-art report documenting increased emphasis in social service and the arts.

The following items are available from the Public Service Materials Center, 355 Lexington Avenue, New York, NY 10017.

Dermer, Joseph. *Where America's Large Foundations Make Their Grants,* 1980.
Lists over 750 foundations, and most but not all of their grants. Arranged alphabetically by state, with grants listed by subject area. Includes deadlines.

Dermer, Joseph. *How to Get Your Fair Share of Foundation Grants,* 1973.
Tells what is expected in a proposal, how to research and approach foundations, based on advice of nine experts in the field.

Dermer, Joseph. *How to Raise Funds from Foundations,* 1973.
    Offers help in avoiding common pitfalls and suggests planning procedures and
    approaches that have worked well for others. Includes an especially useful section on
    resuming contact with a foundation that has initially turned you down.
Foundations that Send Their Annual Reports, 1976.

For those of you interested in foundations outside the United States,
check out the following directories, both of which list foundations by
country and will give you information similar to the Foundation
Center's *Foundation Directory.*

Directory of European Foundations. New York: Basic Books. (updated periodically)
    Pinpoints American organizations that receive funds from foundations in Europe.
International Foundation Directory. Detroit: Gale Research Co. (n.d.)
    Foundations in more than 40 countries are described.

Additional information on foundations that fund specific areas of
interest are also available, sometimes from national organizations and
associations. For example, you might want to check the following
items, some of which may lead you to government sources in addition
to foundations.

Robinson, Philip (Ed.), *Foundation Guide for Religious Grant Seekers. Missoula, MT:
    Scholars Press, 1979.*
Millsapps, D. (Ed.), *National Directory of Arts Supported by Business Corporations and
    Foundations.* Washington, DC: Washington International Arts Letter, 1978.
Dodge, A. B., & Tracy, D. (Eds.) *How to Raise Money for Kids.* Washington, DC:
    Coalition for Children and Youth, 1978.
Katzowitz, L. *Researching Foundations.* Los Angeles: Grantsmanship Center, 1978.
Struckoff, E. C. *The Handbook of Community Foundations: Their Formation,
    Development and Operation.* Washington, DC: Council on Foundations, 1977.

Directories on foundations that are located in your state are available
from a number of sources. These may be published by the League for
the Human Services or by a state agency. The easiest way to locate the
directory is by contacting the state attorney general's office. This office
is responsible for granting the foundation a license to operate and gives
it the preclearance to operate on a tax-free basis. The governor's office
and a state legislator's office are other places to contact. The book by
Leferts described in Chapter 7 includes a complete list with up-to-date
addresses for state directories.

See also references in Chapters 3, 5, and 6.

Chapter 5

THE BUSINESS OF BUSINESS IS BUSINESS
Seeking Private Sector Funds

VIGNETTE 9: FROM REDLINING TO REDEVELOPMENT

They accused us of redlining. It wasn't true. It is true that the banks were redlining, refusing to provide mortgage or improvement loans to people in high risk neighborhoods. We're an insurance company; we did not see it as in our interest to make mortgage loans. But we were selling insurance in every neighborhood, regardless of the risk. High risk policies cost more; but that's business. We've always had a commitment to the communities in which we have national or regional headquarters. So we were willing to take the risks, even lose money on some of the policies we sold.

Still, as the neighborhoods close to the inner city were deteriorating, costs were getting higher. Some businesses were suffering badly. Boarded up storefronts were a common sight. Thefts increased as some of the more stable residents moved away and as some of the major institutions, the churches and banks, pulled out. A major fire or two seemed to break out every week. We suspected arson in some business establishments and in some deteriorated apartment buildings. And as everyone knows, health problems are most severe in poverty areas. There is no question that neighborhood deterioration was costing us money.

And we did have to close some of our offices or pull out some of our agents. But we never refused a bona fide request for insurance. We weren't redlining, even if that's not how CORP saw it. CORP is a network of neighborhood associations that calls itself the Community Organization and Rehabilitation People. They lumped us together with the banks, picketed our offices, issued damaging press releases. Frankly, it wasn't good for our public image.

And it didn't fit our image of ourselves as a community-spirited company. A number of the executive staff were pretty defensive, wanted to counterattack in the press. Interestingly, the board wasn't defensive at all. We had a number of church, business, and labor people on the board who felt strongly about the attacks on the company. They felt even more strongly about profits. And they believed just as strongly in our social commitments as a company and as an industry. The problem was that profits, image, and commitments seemed to be out of synch. "As you know, the archdiocese provides some support for CORP," one of our board members pointed out. "We know they tend to be seen as extremists, but we've always found them to have done their homework. If they are targeting this company, we should examine the charges seriously."

The board chairman agreed. He established a task force to recommend a course of action. One of its recommendations was to sit with representatives of CORP. I participated in the first meeting. I was empowered to offer CORP a grant for training local residents in community development techniques and for increasing CORP staff. At first they thought we were trying to buy them off.

"Look," I explained, "we are not about to abandon the city. Unstable neighborhoods cost us money, and we are fully aware that they create tragedies for the people in them. If you can help stabilize the neighborhoods, we all stand to gain." They agreed to think on it and we set up a series of planning meetings. At the second session, CORP came in with a number of demands. Money for organizers wasn't enough, they argued. They wanted us to invest in building rehabilitation projects: fixing up homes and redeveloping shopping centers. "Why not use your investment portfolios to reduce your insurance risks?" they asked. They offered to take us on tours of several neighborhoods to show us what was needed and to meet some of the people we would be investing in. We went.

After several more meetings, we agreed to put up $4 million for short-term rehabilitation and new construction loans, if CORP, with our help, could induce banks to put up the money for long-term loans, and if CORP could establish local neighborhood nonprofit corporations to manage each project. It took about six months to put the deal together. CORP insisted we also reopen neighborhood-based insurance offices. We did.

We're now three years into the experiment. None of our loans have defaulted. Once the banks were threatened with law suits for redlining and saw that we were willing to put our money on the line, several agreed to enter into cooperative agreements on long-term financing. From our perspective, the experiment has increased our profits and reestablished our image as a forward-looking, community-oriented company. It's good business.

Income from the sale of policies has grown enormously; and outlays in terms of payments on claims has decreased considerably. Most important, three of the seven neighborhoods we are currently involved in have stabilized, and three of the others seem to be turning around. We may be too late on the seventh, but we've got some new ideas there, too.

NEW PARTNERSHIPS WITH
THE PRIVATE SECTOR:
SOME FACTS,
LOT OF FICTIONS

According to some proponents of the "new federalism," cuts in federal government appropriations to such human service programs and nonprofit organizations as those in the education, culture, and health business, are necessary not only to balance the budget, but to shift the locus of responsibility to the more proximate levels of government and to the private sector. However, states, municipalities, and county governments have not been able to pick up the slack. In many sections of the country, particularly the older industrial areas, a shrinking tax base has resulted in even greater cuts to programs. Let us look at some of the figures.

Mental health service budgets in some states have been cut by as much as 40 percent over a three-year period beginning in 1980. Cuts in Title XX social welfare funds have reduced services to the disabled, to children, to youth, to other disadvantaged populations. Ethnic and racial minorities have been hit the hardest. The voluntary sector, which had revenues of approximately $180 billion in 1980 (about half of which went to educational, cultural, and human service programs) has been on the defensive ever since.

Those revenues had been provided in roughly the following proportions: one-half from user fees or third parties; one-quarter from all forms of charitable giving; and one-quarter from government sources. Government funding for entitlement programs, such as medical care, are difficult to cut. Medical care, moreover, is heavily funded through user fees and third-party insurers. But social service and community development programs, which are funded almost entirely through categorical and discretionary grant programs, are relatively easy to cut. Thus, legal aid services, which were in disfavor with the Reagan Administration suffered disproportionately. Federal budget cuts are expected to cause private and voluntary nonprofit organizations to lose approximately $27 billion between 1981 and 1984, of which $5 billion will be cut from social service programs.

Changes in the tax structure make the situation even more bleak. The 1981 tax reform bill reduced the maximum deduction an individual could take from 70 percent to 50 percent. A donor who in previous years might have made a charitable contribution of $10,000 would have been out of pocket only $3000 since he or she could have deducted 70 percent of that gift. Today a $10,000 donation would put the doner out $5000. The 1981 tax law also lowers the corporate incentive for making charitable contributions by reducing corporate tax liability. Although business enterprises continue to be permitted to contribute up to 10 percent of their pretax profits for charitable purposes, historically the actual amounts given have been a fairly stable 1 percent or less. This percentage is hardly expected to increase without proper incentives. Cumulatively, government cuts and changes in the tax laws are expected to cost nonprofit organizations almost $46 billion by 1984.

To darken the picture even further, any reduction in profits by many major corporations is not likely to induce them to increase charitable contributions. Some of the programs most severely hit by federal cutbacks are among those least popular with business leaders. Legal aid services for the poor, for example, have resulted in a number of public action law suits against corporations. Even with the best of goodwill, business could not easily step into the breach left by organizations that have folded because of inadequate financial support. Businesses at the local level are not likely to have the expertise to do needs assessment, services planning, or to conduct human services programs for people in need. Nor is it their business to do so.

So where are the incentives for the new partnerships between the private and the public sectors or the private and the voluntary sectors? The incentive is not likely to be purely philanthropic. In most situations it will have to be in the direct self-interest of the corporation. The example in the vignette at the start of this chapter is a case in point. The insurance company reduced its payments while increasing its premium income; it made a profitable investment as well.

Partnerships between social agencies or community groups and business enterprises must be true partnerships. Asking for a handout is not the way to build a partnership. Building on the concerns of both partners can be. What follows is a list of other examples that may stimulate you to consider opportunities in your locale.

In Arlington, Virginia, a developer who sets aside a certain percentage of flats for low- and moderate-income families in a middle-income development recieves special dispensation of zoning ordinances governing the height or density of apartment buildings within the development.

In the Detroit area, a mental health center offered to provide drug counseling services to workers in an industrial plant, to be reimbursed in part by a third-party payer (a medical insurer), and later went on to interest the industrial firm in funding prevention programs in the schools where employee's children attend, thus improving productivity and morale in the plant.

In Baltimore, a citizen's movement sparked by the Roman Catholic archdiocese induced the Baltimore Gas and Electric Company to raise $200,000 from the private sector, which the city department of social services distributed to those of the city's poor who could not pay their utility bills. It cost BG&E, but it also saved money by eliminating the need to shut off utilities to those who could not afford to pay their fuel bills. People would have suffered, and the unpaid bills would probably have totalled more than the money raised and distributed.

Food banks in a number of communities throughout the United States have profited as a result of the Tax Act of 1976, which stipulates that corporations may donate equipment or stock to charitable institutions for the ill, for infants, or for the needy. In some cases a social agency may issue vouchers for food that are redeemable at a supermarket. In other cases the supermarket donates dented cans, day-old breads, or slightly wilted vegetables to a distribution center, saving itself money through a tax write-off.

Shared housing arrangements, mediated by a family service agency, resulted in private and public grants for the rehabilitation of several privately owned buildings in a northwest community. The landlords benefited through the program by having needed repairs made to their buildings and by full occupancy, even though they charged reduced rents.

Tax reductions are offered by the District of Columbia to those neighborhood businesses that agree to employ and to train area residents, in particular the young, the elderly, and the disabled.

In St. Louis, a group of business leaders raised several million dollars, which were then matched by the Ford Foundation for the sponsorship of minority business enterprises. These businesses received technical assistance from both the private sector and from voluntary and public agencies. The sponsors benefit from more employment, less crime, and a decrease in other problems that would have resulted in property tax increases.

In many of these examples, the initial idea for the project or program came from staff members or volunteers connected with a social agency. Some of these are what have recently come to be known as nonservice approaches. The term is an unfortunate misnomer. It is intended to imply complementary or alternative services without direct cost to the initiating organization. Thus, in Arlington, the county does not have to build or subsidize as much public housing as might otherwise be needed. In Baltimore, the public welfare department does not have to provide heating subsidies to those who cannot afford to pay their utility bills. Government grants or loans are not needed to launch some of the new business ventures for minorities and other disadvantaged populations in St. Louis, and the technical assistance provided reduces the likelihood of failure or default. The insurance company's support of neighborhood renewal increased resources available while increasing the company's profits.

This is not to suggest that there are no costs involved. Of course there are. But the costs are hidden, often absorbed by the private sector, which benefits in terms of reduced taxes, increased income, or reduced outlays. You can get additional information on these nonservice approaches by writing to the Program for Nonservice Social Welfare Initiatives (SRI International, 333 Ravenswood Avenue, Menlo Park, California 94025) or to Nonservice Initiatives Project (Public Technology, Inc., 1301 Pennsylvania Avenue, N.W., Washington, D.C. 20004).

INVESTIGATING THE OPPORTUNITIES IN YOUR AREA

As these examples suggest, there is no standard way of investigating grants or nonservice contributions by business enterprises in your community. Direct grants to other contributions from corporations do not operate the same way as company foundations. These foundations, where they exist, were established in order to divorce philanthropy from on-going business operations, and by so doing, protected gift giving from fluctuations in corporate income. It unlinked corporate giving from direct corporate interests.

Direct corporate interests, on the other hand, are the key to getting increased support from the private sector. And this should be the focal point of your investigation of opportunities for private sector support and involvement. Universities have operated on this principle for a long time. For the past 35 years or so, one of the primary beneficiaries of corporate philanthropy was educational institutions, particularly universities. The endowment of chairs and the provision of scholarships to prestigious institutions or to local colleges and universities were seen by donors not only as good public relations, but as good business. Corporate contributions resulted in a more highly trained pool of recruits and in research activities that are often of direct benefit to the corporate sponsor.

This limited, although relatively successful, effort on the part of higher education to gain corporate support did not come without considerable effort. Nevertheless, support continues to be ad hoc, isolated, and relatively sporadic and arbitrary. Successful efforts by universities generally depend on successful relationships to a company's chief executive officer and to other management staff. Unfortunately, these managers may not see corporate contributions as being in the company's best interest. Efforts to increase corporate giving have been enhanced somewhat by the Council for Financial Aid to Education, a kind of financial trade association for higher education. Similar trade associations do not yet exist for social welfare agencies, social and community development groups, or other human services. Could you establish one in your community? If you do, remember that it is the private sector's interest, not your agency's, that must be the focal point.

Let's face it. The American public did not buy Chrysler products in 1982 and 1983 because they wanted to enhance the company's profits or because they wanted to bail the company out of a devastating cash flow problem. They bought Chryslers because they were convinced by Lee Iacocca that the company was here to stay, and that it was selling the best product for the price, a product that was well built by a company that was committed to survival. Companies are not about to buy an agency's service for any other reason. Going to an executive officer with hat in hand and with a request for funds because the government is no longer willing to support one of your programs, or because the United Way was not successful in its campaign, is no way to generate enthusiasm.

Company executives are concerned with fiscal responsibility and their responsible stewardship of funds. Commercial enterprises are profit oriented. Proposals we make to them should indicate clearly the financial advantages, in the short or long run, that are likely to accrue to the enterprise. Proposals should include clear definitions of the product, its quality, the procedures to ensure production on time, and the accountability mechanisms used to ensure conformity to acceptable standards.

Company concerns with stewardship mean we have to give evidence that our staff are knowledgeable and qualified to do the job we intend to do, and that our board members are responsible, committed, and respectable individuals.

Finding out which company is willing to buy, and what they may be willing to purchase or to engage in directly, may take a great deal of research. The insurance company/community development and the settlement house/supermarket experiences are fortuitous examples of effective partnerships. You will need to research the business enterprises in your community that will be open to general partnerships that can be of equal benefit to your organization and to the publics it seeks to serve.

There are some standard places to start: The National Committee for Responsible Philanthropy (810 18th Street, N.W., Washington, D.C. 20006) advocates for the needs of nonprofit organizations concerned with social change. The *Independent Sector* is a journal that also advocates for corporate and foundation contributions to voluntary nonprofit organizations, primarily human service organizations. (Its address is the Council on Foundations, 1828 L Street, N.W., Washington, D.C. 20036.) The Public Management Institute (at 333 Hayes Street in San Francisco, California 94102) publishes an annual *Directory of Corporate Philanthropy* with information on the giving programs of the top 500 businesses in America. It also publishes numerous reference works and conducts training and consultation services. The Conference Board (at 845 Third Avenue, New York, New York 10022) also sponsors workshops and publishes reports on major corporate philanthropic policies and practices. You might also write for a list of relevant publications to the American Enterprise Institute in Washington, D.C. This institute has been conducting research, sponsoring symposiums, and publishing policy papers on related topics.

At the end of this chapter I have listed a number of directories that I think you may find invaluable. They list the most important and largest corporations in the country, and often provide information on the locations of each company, the products they produce, the names of key officers, and sometimes their interests and affiliations. You may find the names of some business leaders who are active on boards or organizations like your own, or who may be alumni of the same university you or your board members attended. Look over the list carefully. Hit the library and do some research.

You may prefer to start closer to home. Read the newspapers carefully. Clip out articles on local corporations and businesses and on company executives who are involved in some activity close to the interests of your organization. Examples might include an executive who has adopted children with special needs, a nursing home that is upgrading its equipment, a corporation with a special program for its retired employees, or a company that donated an older computer to a community college. It may have some word processing equipment next year that is begging for a recipient.

Do not limit yourself to what the press covers. Visit a local stock broker. Find out which area companies are doing particularly well or which ones may have been awarded a lucrative government contract. Brokers are also good resources for locating company annual reports that may include references to new products and product lines, philanthropic activities, or the public images a company may wish to project. Those same companies publish newsletters and other house organs that may give you additional information. They may also be willing to carry stories on the things your organization does that may be of interest to the company's employees and to its consumers.

EXERCISE 5.1
LOCATING COMPANY PROSPECTS

(1) Using the suggestions in this chapter and the directories listed under "Suggestions for Further Reading," identify at least five likely private sector prospects for contributions and five other business or professional firms that might be targeted for partnership efforts of some sort. These may include nonservice approaches.

(2) Complete the Private Sector Funding Source Inventory for one corporation and one other type of private sector enterprise. Item 3 refers to products of services (e.g., automobile manufacturer or health care services) that may have some implication for agency needs. Item 4 refers to the firm's needs or interests (e.g., drug counseling or preretirement counseling for employees or opportunities for executives to become integrated into the community). Item 6 might include involvement of officers on social agency boards, interests in the arts, or in population groups such as the elderly or disabled children.

Exercise 5.1
PRIVATE SECTOR FUNDING (OR NONSERVICE) SOURCE INVENTORY

1. Type of Enterprise
   _____ Corporation
   _____ Small Business
   _____ Public Utility
   _____ Professional Firm
   _____ Other _____
   _____

2. Name: _____
   _____
   Address (local) _____
   _____
   _____
   Telephone ( ) _____

6. Executive Officers and Interests
   a. Chief Executive Officer: ____

      Public Service Interests of
      Affiliations _____
      _____

   b. Community Relations
      Officer _____
      Public Service Interest of
      Affiliations _____
      _____

   c. Other (Title) _____
      _____

Address (national head-
quarters) _____   d.   Other (Title) _____

_____

Telephone ( ) _____

3.   Major Products or Services   e.   Other (Title) _____
     That in Some Way Articulate
     with Agency Interests _____   _____

_____   f.   Other (Title) _____

_____

_____   _____

_____   7.   Materials Available
                                        _____ Annual Reports
_____   _____ Newsletters, House Organ
                                        _____ News Stories
_____   _____ Special Project Reports
                                        _____ Other _____
_____

4.   Company Needs or Interests   _____
     that May be Served by the   8.   Actions to be Taken
     Agency _____   a.   Phone contacts _____

_____   _____

_____
                                        b.   Written Contacts _____
_____

_____   _____

5.   Previous or Recent Gifts
     of Funds, Materials or   c.   Interviews or Meetings _____
     Nonservice Activities
     Relevant to the Human   _____
     Services. Include
     Agencies Involved   _____
     a.   _____
                                        d.   Other _____
     b.   _____
                                             _____
          _____
                                   Data Compiled by _____
     c.   _____
          _____   Date: _____

Time now to go back over the chapter and to identify new practice
principles.

EXERCISE 5.2
LISTING OF PRACTICE PRINCIPLES

(1)   Review the practice principles you identified for working with both
      government and foundation sources in Chapters 3 and 4. Which of

these apply to work with the private sector? Which would have to be modified or eliminated?

(2) Identify additional practice principles in this chapter and add those from your experience or those of colleagues.

(3) Draw up a new list of practice principles appropriate to work with the private sector, or add to and modify the set you developed for government and foundation sources. Which of these are (a) universal, (b) apply only to public, (c) foundation, and (d) private sector sources?

REVIEW

Cuts in government funding are not likely to be made up by the private sector, even if boosted by modest increases in foundation funding. Recent changes in the tax structure serve as a disincentive to individuals and corporations to contribute even in the amounts given for philanthropic purposes in recent years. Despite the economy and despite the fact that corporations can gain some tax advantages by contributing up to 10 percent of their pretax profits to qualified nonprofit organizations, the amount given has hovered around or just below the 1 percent mark for many years. There are no indications that this will change in the near future.

Nevertheless, private sector contributions can be increased if they are clearly in the interest of the donor enterprise. Business enterprises are in business to make money, and increased profits can be achieved through increased income or decreased expenditures. Cooperative arrangements with human service and other nonprofit enterprises are likely to be successful if they articulate with these interests of the private sector. A number of examples were given, including some that required direct investments by private sector organizations, those that required contribution of services or of equipment, those that included service to the private sector, and those nonservice activities that required none of these but that resulted in tax or income savings by the company. To a large extent such activities are likely to take place on the initiation and with the creative leadership of the nonprofit organizations who will benefit directly or who may increase benefits to the populations for which they are concerned.

SUGGESTIONS FOR FURTHER READING

Look over some of the following directories. Most are available to your public library or in a university library. Some may be available in the offices of local corporate headquarter.

Directory of Companies Filing Annual Reports with the Securities Exchange Commission, Superintendent of Documents, Government Printing Office, Washington, DC 20402.
Once you have identified a company you are interested in, you can request an individual corporate annual report, which may give you more information than any other publically available source. Updated annually.

Directory of Corporate Philanthropy, Public Management Institute, 333 Hayes Street, San Francisco, CA 94102.
Gives patterns of top 500 corporations. Updated Annually.

Koskowitz, M., Katz, M., & Levering, R. *Everyone's Business Almanac: The Irreverent Guide to Corporate America.* New York: Harper & Row. (n.d.)
Provides information on who owns what and how much they make.

Middle Market Directory, which can be ordered from Dun and Bradstreet, 99 Church Street, New York, NY 10007.
Lists corporations that have a net worth of $500,000 to $1,000,000. Includes name, address, key employees, sales volume, and other pertinent data. Updated annually.

Million Dollar Directory, also available from Dun and Bradstreet.
Contains geographic and alphabetical notations and Standard Industrial Classification codes that identify the types of industry or activities engaged in. Annual.

Reference Book of Corporate Management, published by Dun and Bradstreet, annual.
A potential gold mine of information on corporate managers in America's largest firms, biographic data that can provide clues to interests and affiliations.

Standard Industrial Classification Manual, Superintendent of Documents, Government Printing Office, Washington, DC 20402.
A taxonomy of types of industries and industrial activities that might provide clues to industries that might have common interests with those of your organization.

Standard and Poor's Register of Corporations, Standard and Poor, 345 Hudson Street, New York, NY 10014.
Indicates names and locations of corporations and identified growth trends. Updated annually.

Standard and Poor's Register of Directors and Executives.
Indicates who leading corporate executives are, interests and affiliations, previous corporate histories. Best used in conjunction with *Register of Corporations* and with *Standard Industrial Classification Manual.*

The Fortune Double 500 Directory, New York: Time and Life Books, Rockefeller Center.
One thousand corporations are listed in rank order according to a variety of economic indicators (profits, employees, etc). Annual.

The Handbook of Corporate Social Responsibility: Profiles of Involvement, Radnor, PA: Human Resources Network, Chitlin Books, 1977.
Names corporations and suggests approaches to use with them.

Thomas Register of American Manufacturers, Thomas Publishing Company, One Penn Plaza, New York, NY 10001. Eleven volumes.
Lists include products and services according to geographic regions, also manufacturers — their contacts, major officers, products, subsidiaries, and affiliates. The manufacturers' association in your state may publish additional directories. Check with your local chamber of commerce or state commerce department for the address.

There are also a number of books that can help you in your search. Most do not deal exclusively with corporations or with the private sector. Check the references in other chapters and at the end of this book for more general texts on fund raising and on grantsmanship. Check those that focus on the arts, on youth, on the aged, or on some other issue of concern to your organization.

Two recent articles may point you in new directions. These are listed below. You can expect a growing literature on the private sector and its relationship to the human services. Keep your eyes peeled to the professional journals and to conference topics sponsored by your professional association, business groups, the Chamber of Commerce, and so on. Ask members of your board or advisory committee to keep an eye out, too.

Whitcomb, Carol A., & Miskiewitz, Maryann K. "Tapping new resources." *Public Welfare*, Winter 1982.

Opinion Column articles by Decker Anstrom, Donald Schaefer, Phyllis Schless, Charles I. Schottland, Robert L. Woodson. "Can the private sector take up the slack?" *Public Welfare*, Spring 1982.

A brief but loaded manual by Howard Hillman may be all that you need to start the process of identifying, approaching, cultivating, and negotiating with business enterprises for grants and other forms of support. It is available from the Public Service Materials Center, 11 N Central Avenue, Hartsdale, NY 10530. The center publishes other books, pamphlets, and workbooks that you may find helpful.

Hillman, Howard, *The Art of Winning Corporate Grants*, Hillsdale, NY: Public Service Materials Center, 1983.

Check with local medical, dental, legal associations or their state offices for memberships, firms, clinics, and the like. These may be listed in the yellow pages of your telephone directory. Some information may be available from additional directories. Marquis Who's Who, for example, publishes a *Directory of Medical Specialists*, and Marindale-Hubbard publishes a *Law Directory*.

Chapter 6

CIVIC DUTY
Seeking Support from the Voluntary Sector

VIGNETTE 10: "I GAVE AT THE OFFICE"

I guess you could say I grew up with this organization. My dad was an active volunteer with the old Community Chest between the world wars. The Chest became the United Way back in the early fifties; that's when our symbol changed from a red feather to a torch; we still call our campaign the "Torch Drive."

This is a strong United Way town. We believe in the voluntary agencies we support; and the residents in the area have always been pretty generous. I don't mean to say that running a campaign is easy; I was chairman of the campaign committee for five years before I was elected president of the United Way board; and there's plenty of work to be done. But we've routinized the work. There are few surprises. I'll tell you how the campaign works; then I'll tell you how we make our allocation decisions.

The biggest chunk of money we get comes from individuals — about 73 percent of the wage-earning population in this town and a lot of homemakers give to the United Way. We have arranged for all the major companies to establish payroll deduction plans, and we ask workers to pledge a couple of hours a week to a full day's salary to the campaign. We thought we would lose some from this sector when we suffered an economic downturn in the early eighties. Just the opposite; the base shrank a bit, but we pressed home what our agencies did and how they helped the unemployed, so contributions actually rose by 8 to 10 percent each year. It didn't happen without a lot of work.

We have a campaign team in each company; usually it includes top management people, and when there is a union, the union reps. Some companies just pass around the literature we prepare on why funds are needed and what everyone's "fair share" might be. But where we have good volunteers, they actually hold meetings or use coffee break periods to interpret our agencies and what we do. About half the money we raise comes from company employees. These are small gifts, but in

*accumulation, they amount to nearly $6 million. We do even better with
employees in government and in nonprofit organizations in terms of
individual contributions. We don't do as well as we could from such
independent professionals as attorneys and doctors and insurance agents.
Next year we'll borrow a strategy long employed by some of the sectarian
fund-raising federations such as the Jewish Welfare Federation and
Catholic Charities. We'll have doctors soliciting other doctors in their own
specialties, and so on.*

*Altogether about two-thirds of the money we raise comes from individuals,
including homemakers and retired people who we get to through
neighborhood door ringing campaigns, and through the mail.*

*We also get another 25 percent of our funds from major companies. This
is an area we could stand some improvement in. Most of the companies
that donate, give us between 2 and 4 percent of their pretax profits. But
only about 12 companies account for more than half of what we raise in
corporate gifts. Most companies don't give anything, even though the law
allows gifts of up to ten percent. We also get about three percent of our
money from small businesses, another place we could stand to improve.
And every year the community foundation donates around $2.5 million,
just above 2 percent of what we raise. The foundation and some of the
corporations earmark their funds to specific agencies or projects. A few of
the individual donors do too. But, by-and-large, we make the determination
of how the money gets allocated and to whom. The process is also
routinized and that's why it is so cost-efficient.*

*We have six allocation divisions. Each division has about sixty volunteers
on it. We try to make sure those volunteers include board members and
others who have been active with some of our member agencies, the ones
to whom we allocate moneys. We also have professionals from those
agencies on the division committees.*

*Each division deals with a particular service area. For example, the Family
Service Division deals with family counseling, child guidance, adoptions and
foster care, and so on. The Health Care Division deals with drug and
other forms of substance abuse services, with community health clinics, and
we've become affiliated with local chapters of the American Cancer Society,
and the American Heart Association with whom we do joint campaigns.
We also have an Education and Recreational Division, a Cultural Arts
Division, a Legal Aid, Protection, and Safety Division, and a Community
Development Division. Our Volunteer Recruitment and Training Program is
handled separately.*

*Each division has a chairperson and several committees. One committee
reviews staff-prepared reports on needs and previous allocation patterns. It
sets target figures for allocations for the current year. Other committees
review the specific allocation requests of member agencies and of other
petitioner organizations that are not full members but that provide a
service that falls under one of our priorities.*

*If it were just a matter of looking at each agency's request and dividing
up the pie, it would be relatively easy. But it's more than that. Agencies
have to come in and make their pitch to each of the subcommittees,
justifying their expenditures and in particular any deviation from last*

year's expenditures. In some cases we try to induce an organization to move aggressively into a new area. No one was doing drug counseling with teenagers, for example. So we targeted two member agencies we thought should and could. We negotiated with them for some time, even threatened to cut back some funds from what we thought were nonessential services, at the same time that we offered the carrot of increasing funding if they moved into drug counseling.

The carrot-and-stick method sometimes works, but we try to stay on the carrot side. We study problems, involving agency staff and volunteers in the study process. The United Way planning and technical assistance staff helps the member agency prepares a proposal for a new or expanded service. So when their request comes in, it is something we have already all but agreed should be done.

The problems occur when an agency is doing things that are no longer relevant. It's hard to phase out a member agency or pressure it to change. Their board people and staff are after all on our division committees and boards, too. And if they aren't they've got other supporters who may be.

It can also be difficult for a new organization to get United Way support. We have a pretty high set of standards for professional practice. And a new organization will have to follow our budgetary procedures, agree to limit its own independent fund-raising efforts, and will have to engage in activities that the division and the board consider high priority items.

The Rape Prevention Center is an example in point. It started as a volunteer-run self-help group. It applied for funding for the first time four years ago. But rape prevention was not on our list of priorities at the time, nor were we convinced that the center had the capability of doing what it claimed. So we established a time-limited task force that included members from the Health Care and Family Service and Community Development Divisions to study the extent of the problem and to recommend whether or not rape prevention or counseling services were needed in town, whether these should be conducted under existing agency auspices, whether the center was the right organization to do it, and if so, from which divisions should the allocation be made. The study process took two years, but in the meantime, the task force recommended an emergency allocation of $2500 a year out of the board's contingency fund to carry the center while its request was being studied.

You've heard the expression, "I gave at the office." And when it comes to money, most people do. But as you can see, they give a lot more in time and in commitment. In addition to volunteering for committee and campaign work, we have about 850 people affiliated with the Volunteer Bureau through which they get training and are referred to member agencies. They give at the office, but it may not be their own.

VIGNETTE 11: ALL FIRED UP

About a year ago, we found ourselves in deep difficulty. Not only was our growth threatened by cuts in federal and state grants, and by reduced access to philanthropic foundations, but the organization's very survival as a health advocacy center was in danger. The problems were not of our own making. Shifts in national and regional spending priorities and a lagging economy had conspired to define our services as nonessential. But the staff was not about to accept that definition. If the problems were not of our own making, we decided, the solution would be.

One of our major concerns was the prevention of disabling, disfiguring, and life-threatening burns. "It is precisely when times are bad that we have to get our act together," Marvin Kligman, our director, began a staff meeting. "Cuts or no cuts, this is the time when public awareness and prevention activities are all the more important." "Clearly we can't do it all alone," I found myself responding. "Right," Marv continued. "Up to now we depended on others for grants and contracts. We're still going to have to depend on others for financial resources, but we are going to have to find new ways of getting the money we need. Let's make a list of those groups and organizations in the community that might care as much about burn prevention as we do."

The list generated by staff included fire fighters; the police; public health officials; individuals, physicians, nurses, and health care professionals; public housing officials; landlords; and a number of other easily definable publics. "Okay," continued Marv, "let's figure out which of these are to be targets of our intervention, and which ones are potential partners in that intervention." Staff members discussed each public. Some, such as landlords, were both targets and potential collaborators. But landlords were not likely to put money out or engage in a fund raiser on behalf of the institute. Health care providers might be individually concerned with prevention and with treatment, but were also not likely to be actively engaged in fund-raising activities. Fire fighters, on the other hand, seemed to be a good bet for involvement as partners in raising the public's consciousness as well as suppliers of needed financial resources.

When I first approached one of the fire fighters' associations, I was surprised at the warmth with which they greeted me. I've never really known firemen. Let me tell you, they know their business and they care. They depend on each other in emergencies, they develop a real camaraderie and esprit de corps. And they have no trouble including other people in their inner circles. That's why they are so outgoing and friendly toward school kids when they come to visit the firehouse. And most of all, they know what getting burned means.

The first thing that we did was to provide them with some of our written material on the prevention of fires, handouts that they could use in schools and public presentations. Then we coached them on how to work with the local radio station and the newspapers. But we also leveled with them about our own financial needs. We couldn't continue providing materials of this sort or consult with them without some financial support from the community. I really wasn't expecting it, but the first fund-raising effort took place at their annual picnic last May. Fire fighters and their families, other city officials, and interestingly, people who had been helped by the fire department at one time or another, were all there. The chief got up and made a speech, then he introduced me. I spoke for about five minutes about how we all need to work together and I described some of the serious consequences of burns to individuals and their families. The chief *came back to the mike and told everybody about the importance of the work of our institute and asked everybody to dig in. I hate to get cute about it, but they were really "fired up." They collected over $500. The firefighters were ecstatic.*

When I met with them a few weeks later, they felt proud of themselves, but as one of the guys put it, "We really can do better but we don't know much about fund raising." That was my opportunity. Together we mapped out a campaign that included the involvement of parent/teacher organizations, the same PTOs with which the firefighters worked when schools sent children to visit the fire stations in the community. And it included involving burn victims as well as people who had suffered property damage but not bodily harm through fires.

It took only about three months of organizing to put everying in place. The annual picnic is now seen as a fund-raising event. They are about to start a semiannual letter-writing campaign. The fire fighters' wives auxiliary has opened up a thrift shop (and would you believe, it got its first major donation from what was left over in a clothing store after a fire).

It turns out that several of the fire fighters were active members of their local Kiwanis and Knights of Columbus chapters. They have started pressing for those organizations also to raise money for burn victims. Most of these dollars will probably stay in the community, but some may be directed to supporting some of the institute's activities, at least to purchasing some of our written materials.

This year we expect about $2500 in gifts from that community, but that is not the entire point. By involving people in fund-raising efforts, we have actually involved them in a process of consciousness-raising. I've spent about twenty working days in that community, and I suppose from a fund-raising effort that wouldn't be cost effective. Not the first time around. But it will get more cost effective as the community is able to take on more and more responsibility for fund raising on our behalf. And as we get more experienced with these approaches, we will be able to replicate them in communities throughout the country. We couldn't have found better partners than the fire fighters.

FUNDING THROUGH THE VOLUNTARY SECTOR

Until the advent of the New Deal in Roosevelt's first term, the vast majority of social services and most of the cultural arts programs in the United States were funded almost exclusively by the private and voluntary sectors. Family service agencies, settlement houses, Ys and community centers, child guidance clinics, sheltered workshops (e.g., Goodwill Industries, the Salvation Army), and others either raised their own funds through local and national campaigns, or joined forces with other agencies in federated campaigns.

Although many voluntary agencies also get government support (through contracts and grants) and foundation support (through endowments and grants), most continue to depend on all or substantial support from federated campaigns. By far the largest and most ubiquitous of the fund-raising organizations in the United States and Canada is the United Way. Other sectarian or ethically oriented campaigns include those conducted by Jewish Welfare Federations, Catholic Charities, the Urban League, Lutheran Social Services, and so on. Which sectarian federations exist in your community? Are there other federated structures that raise funds for a particular sector of the community: an arts council, a hospital or health federation? Some campaigns, particularly for the health and environment issues, may be national in scope.

In recent years voluntary agencies and other nonprofit organizations have begun to develop effective partnerships with different kinds of voluntary associations. Some agencies develop a fund-raising arm, sometimes called an *auxiliary* or the *Friends of . . . ,* but I am not referring to these. I am referring to the various civic and fraternal organizations in the community — the Order of the Eagles, the Elks Club, the Masonic Lodge, the Knights of Columbus, the Royal Order of the Moose. To these you might add groups like the Jaycees, Council of Jewish Women, local chapters of the National Organization of Women (NOW), environmental groups, the Junior League, and other associations that are purely local in character such as a local chamber of commerce. These are often referred to as *service clubs.* Check the yellow pages and various local directories for them. You are also likely to find churches, synagogues, and other religious organizations listed, as well as booster clubs, educational organizations, and advocacy groups. Which of these are likely partners in fund raising? From which are you likely to get grants or allocations on an occasional or regular basis? Through which of these could you make connections with larger corporate givers?

The industrial unions are a not unlikely source of support. Even in times of high unemployment, when unions are themselves hard pressed for money, they invest considerable sums in social services for their members, for retired members, and for former members who may be currently unemployed. Unions also have large trust funds through which they sometimes make modest but nevertheless significant gifts, particularly if these gifts result in benefits to the union's members.

How could your agency's services increase the union's bargaining position during its next round of negotiations with industry? For example, when unions were first considering negotiating for mental health benefits, they were in desperate need of service providers with whom they could contract on an experimental basis to test out alternative ways in which those benefits might be structured. What are the hot issues today in your community?

THE UNITED WAY:
A PROTOTYPE "FEDERATED" STRUCTURE

There are over 2200 independent and autonomous United Ways in the United States; Each is loosely affiliated with the United Way of America, a national standard-setting and coordinating body. Each is incorporated as a tax-exempt, 501(c)(3) charitable organization governed by its own board of volunteers.

According to an April 1983 fact sheet entitled, "Basic Facts about the United Way" (available from the United Way of America, United Way Plaza, Alexandria, Virginia 22314),

Contributions to United Ways result in financial support for about 37,000 agencies and service groups providing human care services. Literally millions of people are helped each year by the services supported by United Ways.

United Way volunteers of different ages and incomes and from all segments of the community govern their United Way by serving on boards and committees; plan and conduct the annual fund-raising drive; study human service needs and patterns of service delivery; determine priority needs in their community; review agency services and budgets in order to allocate contributions in a fair and efficient manner.

United Ways rank among the most efficient of all charitable organizations. Latest available statistics show the average administration, allocation, and fund-raising cost of all United Ways is approximately 10 percent of available dollars.

About 4100 professional staff members, according to a 1982 survey, are employed by United Ways and United Way of America to support the work of a far greater number of volunteers. Professional staffs of United Ways range in size from about 150 staff members or more in the largest cities to one in smaller communities. In addition, there are literally hundreds of small, local United Ways run entirely by volunteers.

One thousand two hundred and two independent local United Ways are members of United Way of America, the national association, as of March 1983. Dues contributed voluntarily enable United Way of America to provide programs, services and materials in the areas of training, planning, allocations, government and labor relations, fund raising, communications, national agency relations, and research and data collection.

A breakdown of total allocations by all United Way organizations reporting allocations by services shows the following percentages of support: Family Service — 26.2%; Social Development — 20.6%; Health — 17.9%; Recreation — 6.7%; Neighborhood and Community Development — 8.3%; Protection and Safety — 6.9%; Daycare — 5.0%; Jobs and Income — 3.9%; Education — 2.6%; Other — 1.9%.

Local United Ways are a major source of support for agencies engaged in health services delivery, health research, and health education. In 1982, approximately $245 million, or 17.9 percent of United Way allocations went to such causes.

A total of 7.4 percent of United Way allocation is distributed to agencies which are minority controlled — over half of all volunteers and staff being minorities.

United Ways support services for people from all walks of life and all income groups. Services of United Way-supported agencies often viewed as "middle class" or "traditional" reach heavily into the inner-city and ethnic or lower-income neighborhoods. For example:

— Settlement houses and neighborhood centers received $56 million from United Ways in 1982...a majority of the people they serve being nonwhite and poor.
— Seventy-five percent of Boys Club members come from families with incomes of less that $12,000...44 percent come from families with incomes of less than $8,000, and 13 percent come from families with incomes under $4,000...46 percent are from single-parent families.

Types of services supported by local United Ways include adoption, advocacy, adult education, alcoholism services, arts and culture, child protection, community health clinics, consumer protection, crime prevention, day care, drug abuse services, emergency assistance and shelter care, first aid, foster care, health research, home and mobile meals, homemaker services, individual and family counseling, information and referral/hotlines, job training, legal aid, maternal and child health, mental health education, rape relief, recreation, rehabilitation services, services for handicapped, services for older Americans, services for women, social adjustment, development and functioning, special transportation, suicide prevention, volunteerism [Reprinted by permission of the United Way].

Although smaller United Ways and sectarian or sectorally limited federations may be entirely operated by volunteers, the medium- or larger-sized organizations are likely to have well-trained staff. These include social planners (often with social work background), fund raisers, accountants, and specialists in particular practice sectors or arenas (health, the arts, community development, and the like). Some have professionally managed volunteer bureaus. The fund-raising pattern described in the first vignette is typical of most United Ways. Other federations may rely more heavily on mail and personal campaigns targeted at a more limited segment of the community (e.g., Jews, Catholics, Blacks, or others who support services to targetted groups).

Those large enough to have paid staff all use relatively similar allocation procedures. Councils or divisions are set up to deal with specific areas of interest: cultural and educational programs, social services, health programs, and so on. Each council is made up of volunteers who may have undergone some training before being appointed to the council, or who may have worked on a variety of tasks and on subcommittees prior to their appointments. Each council receives technical assistance from one or more professional staff persons.

The staff also works with "petitioner organizations," those who will be requesting funds to be allocated by the council. This "technical assistance" in the preparation of funding requests is intended to make certain that proper allocating procedure is used and that funding requests are in line with overall funding priorities; these are set by the board, which relies on staff to provide it with information on community needs, particularly those unmet by other sources.

In general, only member agencies can expect to receive an appropriation and this appropriation is made on an annual basis. Member agencies come to expect regular appropriations, generally at the same level as the sums received in the previous year, adjusted for inflation. They are held accountable for the way in which those funds are spent; most report on their programs and spell out the details if their current requests diverge in any way from the previous year's. It is difficult for nonmember organizations to receive allocations.

Nevertheless, such allocations are sometimes made, particularly when the community faces a particularly pressing problem, and none of the member agencies are prepared or willing to take on responsibility. A grant or allocation to a nonmember organization may also be made on a tentative basis if that organization is being tested for possible full inclusion as a member of the federation. In addition to their regular allocations, member organizations may submit requests for the financing of special, innovative projects. Sometimes the funds requested are designated as seed money and are intended to attract funds from other sources. In a period when the available supply of funds seems to be outdistanced by need, federated agencies are examining their traditional allocation patterns very closely. It has, on occasion, become more difficult for old-time member organizations to receive allocations than it is for new organizations that are more responsive to current needs.

On the average, United Ways allocate about 10 percent of the funds raised to their own administrative costs. These include expenditures incurred in the campaign itself, in planning and coordinating activities, in research and evaluation, in bookkeeping and in management of the allocation process, and in volunteer training and placement. By any measure this cost is modest. It compares extraordinarily well with the inefficiencies of fund raising efforts in prefederation days when each agency used to conduct its own fund-raising efforts. Sometimes costs got as high as 80 percent of the amount raised. Local Jewish federations are even more efficient, generally allocating less than 8 percent of the money raised to campaigns and related administrative costs.

United Ways perceive themselves as leaders in promoting sound accounting and financial reporting principles. *Accounting and Financial Reporting, A Guide for United Ways and Nonprofit Human Service Organizations* was first published in 1974. It is still one of the best guides available. It contains standards, models, and directions for use by United Ways in reporting expenditures and income *and* identifying expenditures and income of the agencies to which the monies are allocated. According to the United Way, "based on the latest accounting principles of the American Institute of Certified Public Accountants, this guide has become the standard for the nonprofit field. United Ways are committed to full and fair disclosure of all expenses."

The financial records of almost all United Ways are audited annually by an independent public accountant whose examination conform to generally accepted standards outlined in the accounting guide. All United Ways are encouraged to publish financial reports to the public that provide full disclosure of all revenues (including campaign results) and expenditures.

CIVIC GROUPS AND OTHER LOCAL PARTNERS

Fund raisers have too often neglected the potential of establishing partnership relationships with civic and religious organizations. That is why I chose to include the second vignette in this chapter. I do not mean to suggest that your basic support is likely to come primarily from partnerships with any of these groups. That is unlikely. The health care institute in the example certainly did not. By any measure, the amount it raised, even for one of its programs — burn prevention — was relatively modest. Efforts to replicate the pattern described in other communities might increase those funds, but again, not without a good deal of investment. That investment, however, had other programmatic payoffs. By engaging fire fighters first, and then local civic groups, the institute staff was actually able to engage in its primary concern:

heightening public awareness and raising community consciousness of a severe and dangerous problem.

I had occasion to discuss this experience with the institute's staff only a few weeks before writing this chapter. Several practice principles emerged from the discussion. I highly recommend them to any organization. First among these is to *broaden your base of support* so as to minimize your dependency on one or two sources. When foundation grants become scarce, for example, it may make more sense to seek support from industry or the general public, rather than another foundation. Second, *find another partner or partners,* persons and organizations that will be as concerned as you about raising the necessary funds — partners who may even take on fund raising for your organization as a major commitment. Third, *use fund-raising activities in such a way as to complement other organizational programs* and services. In some cases, fund-raising activities may themselves become essential services, particularly when they increase public awareness and involve the public in programs of self-help.

Can you think of others?

Use the inventory form that follows to collect and record information on appropriate voluntary sources of support.

EXERCISE 6.1
FINDING INFORMATION ON VOLUNTARY
FUNDING SOURCES

(1.) Look over the Voluntary Sector Funding Source Inventory. Notice that there are two parts of the form. Form A deals with federated fund-raising and allocating bodies such as the United Way and sectarian organizations. Form B deals with civic associations that may engage in charitable work, but are not necessarily in the funding business. Decide on one federated structure and one civic association you want to know more about.

(2.) Fill in the inventory for each type of organization. You may be able to get all the information you need from the United Way office, or from the local Chamber of Commerce, which may have a list of civic associations. If you are not sure where else to begin, try the Yellow Pages.

Exercise 6.1
VOLUNTARY SECTOR FUNDING SOURCE INVENTORY
Form A. Federated Structures

1. Type of Federated Structure
    _____ United Way
    _____ Sectarian _____
    _____ Other _____
    _____
2. Name of Organization _____

    Address _____
    _____
    Telephone ( ) _____
    _____
3. Major Allocations Division
    a. Arena _____
        _____
        Staff Person _____
        _____
        Lay Leader _____
    b. Arena _____
        _____
        Staff Person _____
        _____
        Lay Leader _____
        _____
    c. Arena _____
        Staff Person _____
        _____
        Lay Leader _____
        _____
    d. Arena _____
        _____
        Staff Person _____
        Lay Leader _____
4. Other Relevant Staff Members
    and Titles of Lay Leaders
    a. _____
        _____
    b. _____
        _____

5. Types of Organizations to
    Which Awards Are Made
    _____
    _____
    _____
6. Types of Allocations Avail-
    able for Nonmembers, if any:
    _____
    _____
7. Membership Requirements or
    Procedure for Becoming
    Members _____
    _____
    _____
8. Total Amount of Funds
    Available
    for Current Year _____
    Specific Divisions _____
    Nonmembers _____
    Other Category _____
9. Current Priorities _____
    _____
    _____
10. Restrictions, if any _____
    _____
11. Funding Cycle: _____
    Campaign Dates _____
    Allocation Dates _____
    Other _____
12. Allocation Procedures and
    Key Dates _____
    _____
13. Materials Available
    _____ Application Kit
    _____ Summaries of Previously
          Funded Projects
    _____ Guidelines
    _____ Sample Proposals
    _____ Other _____

c. _____   **14. Actions to be Taken**
   _____   a. Phone Contacts _____
d. _____
   _____   b. Written Contacts _____
e. _____
   _____   c. Interviews or Meetings _____
f. _____
   _____   d. Other _____
g. _____

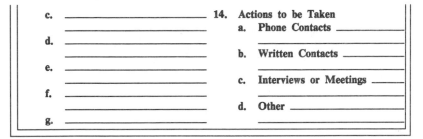

Exercise 6.1
Form B. Civic Associations

1. Type of Association
_____ Fraternal
_____ Business
_____ Ethnic or Sectarian
_____ Church Related
_____ Other _____

2. Name of Association _____
_____

Address _____
_____
_____

Telephone ( ) _____

3. Officers (Names, Titles, Phone Numbers)
_____
_____

4. Other Relevant Contacts and Their Interests

5. National or State Affiliation _____
_____

6. Kinds of Activities Engaged in by Local Chapter that May Be Relevant to Your Organization's Fund Raising Concern
_____

7. National Fund Raising Priorities _____
_____
_____
_____
_____

8. Restrictions, if any _____
_____
_____
_____

9. Other Local Fund Raising Efforts _____
_____
_____

10. Areas of Your Organization's Concern that Might Also Become the Association's Concerns: _____
_____

11. Actions (to be) Taken
   a. Phone Contacts _____
   _____
   b. Written Contacts _____
   _____
   c. Interviews or Meetings _____
   _____
   d. Other _____

```
  _____        _____
  _____        | Inventory  Completed  by:      |
  _____        |                                |
  _____        | Date: _____|
  _____        |                                |
  _____        |_____|
```

RELATIONSHIPS IN
THE ESTABLISHMENT OF PARTNERSHIPS

The extent to which your organization will be successful in getting an allocation for a federated structure or in inducing a civic association to direct some of its fund-raising and charitable activities in your direction will depend on the way your organization and its capacities are perceived. Let us go back to looking at the United Way as a case in point.

The United Way has carved out a domain for itself. In part, this is an historical domain, clearly understood by all concerned. In part, the domain it deals with is a result of the decisions of its current board and its member agencies. "These are the organizations and programs we fund," explained a United Way executive. "There are certainly other worthwhile causes, but if we took them all on, we would dilute our effectiveness and do damage to the member agencies who depend on us. When our priorities shift in response to new needs, if our member agencies aren't willing to shift some of their services, we may look for an outside organization and even give it conditional associate membership. Sometimes an outside petitioner is successful in convincing our staff and board that we are not adequately dealing with newly identified needs. That doesn't mean that the organization that pointed up the shortcomings is the one that is going to get funded. We're going to look at the capacity of an organization to do the job for which we allocate money, the people it serves, and who else might be able to deliver the same product for less money. Most of our member agencies have carved out their own turfs and whatever competition may exist between them is kept to a minimum. When a new organization comes around, it sometimes upsets the domain claims already accepted by those who are affiliated with us."

What your organization actually does, constitutes its de facto domain, although it may also make claims for expanded domain over other problems, populations, or services in the future. That is, it may position itself to take advantage of changing public awareness or emerging problems in a given area of service.

The extent to which it is likely to receive funding for maintaining partial or absolute ownership over its particular turf will depend on the consensus by other relevant publics that its claim is a legitimate one. The United Way must agree that your organization's claim is appropriate and that you have the capacity to perform adequately. Consumers must consider your organization to be the right address to which to apply for service. Collaborating organizations must be willing to work with your organization, even if there may be some competition between your agency and those collaborators over one or more aspects of your claim. These are the variables you will have to demonstrate when applying for membership or associate status to a federated structure.

Domain consensus defines and sets the boundaries and the jurisdiction of your organization within the larger human services community. It includes formal agreements between your organization and others, and informal expectations that services will be provided in an acceptable manner. Consensus over your organization's domain continues so long as the agency fulfills the functions judged to be appropriate to it and adheres to generally agreed-upon norms regarding standards of quality.

For funders to agree that your organization is worthy of support, they will also need to know something about the severity of the problems to be addressed. They must agree that the population to be served is legitimately in need of those services and that the services rendered are appropriate to those needs. Effective claims to domain reflect the credibility an agency has achieved with its input and output publics. Some agencies may be regarded with mistrust, not because of anything they may or may not have done, but because some of its other publics may be mistrusted. Thus, clients may mistrust a social agency because it receives support from a source it does not trust. Some funding sources may not trust a service organization that provides services to consumers that may be considered somehow illegitimate.

An organization's credibility often depends on the credentials of the staff. The way in which these credentials are established will vary from one constituent group to another. "When I first introduced myself to United Way officials," reports the director of an agency, "I established my identity through formal credentials. I interpreted the functions of my agency, and let them know what my responsibilities are. In that first meeting, they couldn't care a hoot about who I was personally, but they did care who I represented and about my, and the agency's, past record. It also helps that I have a Ph.D. It's only after we got to working together, that we developed personal relations, mutual obligations that we were both able to build on.

"But it's different when I meet with representatives of civic associations and other community people," she continues. "They don't want to know about my position in the bureaucracy. They want to know what I stand for, personally, who I am as a person. Even more important is who my organization serves: what the needs of those people are. They are less interested in the services and how they are delivered, than in the needs to be addressed." And perhaps even more important, is the ability of your organization to find common interests with the association and its key members — make your cause their own.

EXERCISE 6.2
LISTING OF PRACTICE PRINCIPLES

(1.) Review your last list of practice principles. It should articulate with your fund-raising efforts directed at government, foundation, and private sector sources.

(2.) Identify additional practice principles in this chapter, and add those from your experience or those of colleagues who have worked with the voluntary sector.

(3.) Draw up a new list of practice principles appropriate to fund raising with the voluntary sector, or add to and modify the master list you have already developed. Which of these principles apply only to the voluntary sector?

REVIEW

The voluntary sector is made up of all those organizations that raise money for charitable or community improvement purposes and those that provide services on a nonprofit basis. Although such voluntary agencies as community centers, a museum, and a local health clinic may raise their own funds through campaigns and other activities, many are affiliated with federated fund-raising and allocating structures. Foremost among these is the United Way. In addition, some belong to sectarian federations or federations organized to respond to the needs of particular populations or to deal with clearly identified sets of programs (health, rehabilitation, and so on). Some voluntary agencies also seek effective partnerships with civic associations. These groups include the Elks, a "boosters" club, a church affiliated group, or the Junior League, and so on.

The United Way is not only prototypic of other federated structures, but is the largest and most ubiquitous of all. There are more than 2200 autonomous United Ways in the United States, the vast majority of which are affiliated with the United Way of America, which is a standard-setting and technical assistance organization to its local affiliates. United Ways are governed by locally elected boards, conduct annual campaigns, determine priority needs in the community, and allocate funds to member agencies and to others who may be designated as affiliates or recipients. Allocation decisions are generally made by lay persons who examine applications and proposals that are groups under various councils or divisions (education and culture, family services, health, and so on).

Many United Ways and other federated structures have highly trained professional staffs who conduct planning, fund raising, technical assistance, accounting, evaluation, and other functions. The allocation and request processes are generally highly structured. Allocations are made only after considerable study.

The relationships between nonprofit service organizations and the wide variety of civic associations that exist in every American community are much more loosely patterned. They vary from partnership to partnership and community to community. The example of a preventive health institute working first through a fire fighters association, and then through the fire fighters to involvement of three other civic groups is an interesting one. It suggests how creativity and the right mixing of mutual interests between organizations and organizations and their members can result in financial support. Just as important, the fund-raising activities serve to heighten public awareness of a problem and public involvement in dealing with the problem, very possibly the programatic objectives of the organization seeking new sources of funds.

SUGGESTIONS FOR FURTHER READING

Start off with some directories.

The Directory of the United Way of America is updated each year and can be ordered from the United Way of America, United Way Plaza, Alexandria, VA 22314.

The National Directory of Private Social Agencies is available from Croner Publications at 211-05 Jamaica Avenue, Queens Village, NY 11428.

Trustees of Wealth: A Taft Guide to Philanthropic Decision Makers is available from the Taft Information System, Taft Products, Inc., 1000 Vermont Ave. NW, Washington, DC 20005.

This guide identifies some of the wealthiest philanthropists in the United States, the kinds of organizations they are affiliated with, their philanthropic interest, and so on. It might be a good place to seek information on persons in your community who are active in federated structures and in civic associations.

Eckstein, Burton. *Handicapped Funding Directory.* Oceanside, NY: Research Grant Guides, 1978.

Provides information about laws pertaining to equality for handicapped persons, publications issued by various organizations dealing with various aspects of the subject, and sources of funding for pertinent projects.

Check also the *Directory of Directories* and the *Directory of Associations* in your public library. It may lead you to other important national addresses that might be good sources of information. The following are among the thousands found in the *Directory of Associations.*

Council of Jewish Federations, 555 Lexington Ave., New York, NY 10017

Family Service Association of America, 44 E. 23rd Street, New York, NY 10010.

Mental Health Materials Center, Information Resources Center for Mental Health and Family Life Education, 419 Park Avenue South, New York, NY 10016.

National Association for the Education of Young Children, 1834 Connecticut Ave., NW, Washington, DC 20009.

National Association for Mental Health, 1800 N. Kent Street, Rosslyn, VA 22209.

National Association for Retarded Children, Inc., 2709 East, P.O. Box 6109, Arlington, TX 76011.

Sex Information and Education Council of the United States (SEICUS), 1855 Broadwar, New York, NY 10023.

United Way of America, 801 N. Fairfax Street, Alexandria, VA 22314.

Check also the reading suggestions in Chapters 2, 3, 4, and 5 and the more general sources of information in Appendix B.

Chapter 7

GETTING ORGANIZED
Eight Steps Toward Writing a Proposal

VIGNETTE 12: BEING IN PLACE

*Our business is making others successful. In a way, that's what we've
always done. When we started off back in the early 1950s, we were a
groupwork agency, had street corner workers spread out in every
neighborhood in the inner city. Times change, and so have we.*

*For the past couple of years, we've been organizing group homes and
halfway houses for former prisoners, mental patients, and the
developmentally disabled. It's no easy task, but we're trusted in many
neighborhoods. We can build on previous relationships as well as on our
mental health experiences.*

*Believe it or not, even though at some times almost 95% of our funds
came from government sources, we still operate as a voluntary agency, still
get a regular budget from the United Way. And we get other contributions
from churches and service clubs who see us as a first line of defense
whenever a neighborhood finds itself under attack.*

*We've changed plenty over the years, but we never left our neighborhood
roots. Our base is in the neighborhoods and we never turned our backs on
people in need or on the agencies that can help them and upon whom we
depend. So when a number of gangs started organizing around the school
yards last year, we were there. And so were several funding sources, ready
to help us do the job.*

DON'T MOURN FOR ME BOYS,
ORGANIZE

The experience described in Vignette 12 is unusual. It should not be.
Too many social agencies find themselves poorly positioned to take
advantage of new opportunities or to shift gears when one source of
support disappears. Being in the right place at the right time requires

being well organized. Joe Hill, a folk hero of the early labor movement in the United States, cried out to his family and friends just before he died, "Don't mourn for me boys, organize!" Some agencies, even those that have been successful in organizing the disadvantaged, have not learned the lesson for themselves. They have not organized the publics on whom they are dependent.

"They destroyed us," the director of a legal aid clinic for the poor told me. "We were just too successful for them, so they cut our funds once, twice, and the third time we were out." He and his agency did strike out, but not because the pitches were not coming where they should.

He struck out because he was too far off base.

To keep opportunities from becoming predicaments or to turn predicaments into opportunities requires knowing where your home base is and being able to move from it or around it as needed. It requires knowing how to ORGANIZE. To be properly organized requires that you:

- Know your *O*rganization.
- Survey and orchestrate your *R*esources.
- Decide on your *G*oals.
- *A*ssess your position among relevant publics.
- Carve out the appropriate *N*iche for yourself among those publics.
- Get the *I*nformation you need in order to act.
- *Z*ero in on the activities or programs you decide to undertake.
- *E*stablish an action plan for achieving your objectives.

I do not mean to get cute or corny about it, but I have found that it is easy to get caught in specifics and to forget to do what is necessary to get into position in order to raise the funds that are needed from various publics, including those that fund grants and contracts. That is what we will focus on in this chapter, and the word *Organize* is a good reminder of the steps that have to be taken. Let's take each of the letters in O R G A N I Z E one at a time. We'll begin with *O*.

KNOW YOUR *ORGANIZATION*

Knowing your organization is the first step in getting organized. A good place to start may be to examine one or more of the agency's programs. A program is made up of activities — services, promotions, resource development, and management — conducted over time. Agency staff and others often become committed to existing programs and arrangements.

A central fact of organizational life is that many find it easier to keep busy with routine tasks than to take on new functions or to change accustomed modes of behavior. Program planners are often dismayed when some service agency personnel show a calculated opposition to change. While staff do not always verbalize their true feelings, their actions may suggest that they generally prefer to maintain their current structures or modes of operation even when a change will obviously enhance the accomplishment of the organization's stated goals or mission.

The reasons for resistance are many. Being pressured into change by outsiders may result in some loss of face. Under such circumstances, financial incentives to individuals and to agencies may be insufficient inducements, particularly if a change once adopted might result in embarrassment or loss of stature in the event of failure.

Agency administrators may perceive change as an imposition on their personnel and thus disruptive to the management process. Agency personnel may be intent on protecting the advantages they receive by keeping things as they are. Change may require learning new skills and modifying accustomed ways of behaving. Some professional staff members may fear that change will result in an erosion of standards, or will require them to perform tasks that could better be performed by others. Frequently, defenders of the status quo fight against change because of what they perceive to be the public interest. Distinguishing between self-interest and public interest is sometimes extremely difficult.

There are significant psychic costs to change. For some personnel, changing established patterns of practice or adding new functions may mean becoming novices again. It takes a long time to become a master craftsman. Most changes require immediate risks. While not changing may result in eventual erosion of influence or service efficiency and effectiveness, that erosion at least is gradual.

Newer organizations are sometimes more apt to take risks. As agencies grow older, they frequently institutionalize earlier innovations. They establish procedures and formalize rules to ensure predictable behavior and to consolidate whatever gains they may have made. Staff become increasingly concerned with the survival and the growth of the organization in which they have become comfortable, rather than with finding new or even more effective means to reach goals. This is not always the case. Many well-established agencies continue to innovate and seek creative solutions to emerging problems. Unfortunately, this is more the exception than the rule.

There are, of course, other obstacles to change, some of them inherent in the system and rather insidious. An agency may agree to the need for change, but be unable to mobilize necessary resources. At times, resources are rendered inadequate by overly rapid expansion, or by an agency's assumption of commitments beyond its capacity to fulfill. Some agencies are limited by lack of access to new ideas and new technologies.

In addition to resource limitations, there sometimes are sunken costs that limit an agency's ability to move from the status quo. Investment in equipment, as in a medical clinic, or in certain kinds of staffs with specialized training who have become tenured employees, represent commitment to previous conceptions of mission. This investment makes adapting to new circumstances almost impossible.

Agencies may also accumulate obligations and commitments that constrain their behavior. Over the years they may have made promises to other service agencies, to consumers, and to providers. The expectations of others may make it extraordinarily difficult for agencies to change their procedures, their programs, or their services without endangering existing relationships. Needless to say, when such relationships are endangered, an organization is less likely to achieve its goals, and its very existence may be threatened.

Since not too many things can be changed all at once without destroying a working system, it is necessary to be clear about those issues that are most important and those practices or procedures or policies that are in greatest need of change. Even those planners who advocate drastic and sweeping changes must tolerate continuation of many established practices. In every organization there must be an accommodation between the proponents of change and the guardians of tradition. What may seem a massive and sudden change to one, may seem infinitesimal to the other.

2. SURVEY AND ORCHESTRATE YOUR *RESOURCES*

Experienced planners are well aware of the fact that they would have little leverage over those they hope to influence without access to or control over the flow of resources. To begin with, planners need money, time, ideas, and other resources just to do their jobs. No organization can accomplish its mission without access to the minimally required resources. A system's outputs cease — or are severely disrupted — shortly after its inputs are terminated. A change in the number or kind of available resources may also influence an organization to expand or modify its programs or services.

Discussion of agency resources are frequently limited to capital or physical facilities and to financing. But resources can be *any of the commodities or means permitting an organization to accomplish its objectives.* While money and credit and physical facilities may be essential to a particular service, they certainly are not sufficient in and of themselves.

Other resources, more ephemeral and elusive than money or facilities, are just as central to organizational survival and service provision. These include political influence; social standing and prestige; charisma, popularity, and esteem; legitimacy and legality; and personal or organizational energy. Organizations are dependent on various elements in their environments for the input of resources. This dependence is often greatest when an organization is unable easily to obtain resources from alternative elements of the environment.

3. DECIDE ON YOUR *GOALS*

Before deciding on a goal, it will be important for you and others in the organization to determine that a problem exists or that some better state of affairs is possible. A problem may exist in the here-and-now or it may be anticipated in the near future. Review our discussion of assessment in Chapter 2. You will recall that problems may be lodged in a group or population, in the service system, or in the way in which programs are managed internally and externally.

When a problem is perceived as being lodged in a population — an organization's current or potential consumers — it may be defined as a lack of skills, a debilitating attitude, or insufficient and erroneous knowledge on the part of members of that population. For example, consumers may not *know* where to get services, how to apply for them, or even that services exist. Some may not recognize the existence of a disability or may not know that it can be dealt with. Others may not have the *skill* to deal with the problem. Still others may be prevented from dealing with it because of debilitating *attitudes*: fear of facing up to a problem, reluctance to seek help, apathy, or loss of confidence in self.

Consumers are not the only ones whose knowledge, skills or attitudes require changing. For example, funders may not *know* about your organization's programs and capacities. The general public may not be aware of the needs of particular populations (for example, children in need of permanent placements), and other agencies may not know that your organization is willing to accept referrals or enter into collaborative service projects. These potential resource suppliers may also be limited by lack of *skill* in relating to your organization. Similar problems may affect relationships between your organization and others involved in service delivery. For example, a potential collaborator may not follow the appropriate procedures for making referrals (*skill*). Some of its staff may hold inappropriate attitudes about your organization's services (for example, legal aid), or the clients it seeks to serve. It may not even be aware of those services clients need (*knowledge*).

Internal resistance to change or to a new service approach can also be analyzed in the same way. For example, agency staff may not possess the requisite *skills* to serve a lower-income population with drug abuse problems. They may not *know* the severity of the problem or how it affects other services and programs the agency conducts. Or they may be *biased* against certain client groups, defining them as deviants when a more appropriate attitude might be to see them as victims.

In some cases these problems may not be serious at the moment, but shifts in public perceptions, in government policies, or in economic conditions are likely to increase their severity in the future. Let us turn our attention now from populations to services and their priorities.

A useful way to begin might be to focus on the extent to which services are *available, accessible,* and *sufficient.* Sufficiency is sometimes measured in terms of *effectiveness and efficiency.* The neighborhood service organization, described in the introduction to this chapter, was able to take on more functions when it became clear that services were needed but not available from other providers. Sometimes, however, services are available, but they are not accessible. For example, a community mental health center might close its doors at 5:00 p.m., before most neighborhood residents get off work. Another agency might be culturally inaccessible because the technical jargon — the language its practitioners use — is foreign to the population in need of service, or because class differences give the agency an appearance of being a foreign element imposed on the local population.

"A difference that makes no difference, is no difference," Charles Pierce, a nineteenth-century American philosopher, once said. Some services are both available and accessible, but they do not have much of an impact on the lives of recipients. Others are inefficient, costly to both the client and the provider agency in money, in time invested, in opportunities lost. And finally, all too many services are unresponsive to the interests of various publics and are conducted in such a way as to be unaccountable to those who should have some say in their planning, delivery, or evaluation. These concerns are difficult to separate from marginal issues. Nevertheless, some problems are the result of marginal deficiencies.

When management issues are examined, our focus of attention might be internal to the agency itself or external to it. Internal management problems might be defined as low productivity, poor interpersonal relationships, abuse of authority, and lack of innovation. All these are clearly related to the other problems we have been discussing. When attention is focused externally, the concerns might be with the resource development and organization, or continuity, consistency, and comprehensiveness of services.

For example, a mental hospital might have an excellent patient rehabilitation program, but the program becomes ineffective if there is no continuity of care following discharge. An agency might have a perfectly adequate budget, supported from many sources, but may have no guarantee that such support will be available a year or two later. *Comprehensiveness* refers to the extent to which different services complement each other. Suppose a family under stress presents the following issues to an agency: the father is laid off, the mother is an alcoholic, a teenage son has had repeated brushes with the law, a twelve-year-old girl may be suffering from a chronic disease and low self-image, and younger children are doing poorly in school. Services aimed exclusively at one or another of these problems may be ineffective unless others are dealt with at the same time.

In the chart below, I have listed some of the key terms in this discussion. Look them over. How can they help you in defining a problem to be dealt with in your plan or proposal for change?

Focus of Attention	*Issues to be Addressed*
Populations or Individuals	Lack of Knowledge
	Lack of Skill
	Debilitating Attitudes
Services	Availability
	Accessibility
	Effectiveness
	Efficiency $\Big\}$ Sufficiency
	Accountability
Internal Management	Productivity
	Interpersonal Relationships
	Authority
	Innovation
External Management	Continuity
	Consistency
	Comprehensiveness

These terms can also be helpful when you use what we spoke of in Chapter 2 as a normative approach to assessment. The normative approach requires that you begin with some consensus on a desired state of affairs. This vision may emerge from the deliberation of a task force composed of board members, staff, volunteers, and consumers. Or it may be the result of a consultant's recommendations. It might be borrowed from the experiences of like agencies in other communities. It might be embodied in the standards of a professional association with which your organization is affiliated.

Once a normative model has been established, it becomes a standard against which the current reality is examined. For example, in designing a full service family agency you would concern yourself with the types of services to be made available, their accessibility, effectiveness, efficiency, and so on. How close does your agency approximate the desired model?

If you start with a problem approach (here-and-now or anticipatory), you will have to transform the problem statement into a goal statement. If you start off with an anticipatory approach, the goals are embodied in the normative model of practice.

Goals are broad statements of intent and purpose which both energize and legitimate a process. The 1979 edition of *Webster's New Collegiate Dictionary* defines a goal as "the end toward which effort is directed." It is the aim of that effort: the purpose of the actions taken. Goals give direction to the effort. They energize because they give participants a sense of shared purpose, a common target toward which to aim. They legitimate because they explain to others the purpose of those efforts in language that conveys a social good, a general benefit or a benefit to particular populations or organizations that are considered deserving or in need.

Goals are phrased in general terms that cover relatively long time spans. For this reason, they may never be fully reached. Since they serve as energizers and legitimaters, this is perfectly appropriate. It may be desirable for goals to change over time if they are to continue to energize. Like problems, goals can be stated in terms of (1) populations; (2) services, and (3) management. Examples of population-oriented goals include:

- Graduates of the school will be committed to ongoing and continuous education and professional development.

- Community leaders will be aware of the special needs of disabled persons, and committed to their normal integration into all aspect of community life.

Service oriented goals might include the following:

- All children in need will have available to them permanent and supportive family placement.

- A 24-hour suicide and family violence prevention self-help clinic will be established to serve residents in the south central district.

Management oriented goals might include the following:

- A management information system will be introduced to increase access to needed information by all agency staff and collateral providers.
- Rehabilitation services will be provided in a continuous manner, and coordination mechanisms will be established with the schools, the courts, employers, and other relevant organizations.

Objectives are derived from goals. They spell out in performance terms what is intended. Objectives can be viewed as "subgoals," stops along the road to achieving a more general goal. Unlike goals phrased in general terms, the objectives are specific, time-oriented and measurable. Objectives can be phrased in terms of (1) operations, (2) activities, or (3) outcomes. For example, suppose we were to begin with the goal of establishing a 24-hour suicide and family violence prevention clinic. Here are what some of the objectives of the clinic might look like:

- *Operations Objective.* Thirty volunteer staff members will be recruited, trained, and assigned to monitor telephone and walk-in operations in numbers sufficient to handle all requests for service.
- *Activity Objective.* By the end of the first year, four self-help groups will have been organized to operate with minimal assistance from the agency, and between two and six others will be in various stages of development.
- *Outcome Objective.* The rate of repeat suicide attempts in the south/central district will be reduced 25 percent within a twelve-month period.

Any goal statement is likely to generate a number of operational objectives. Some of these will be feasible within the limitations of the agency, its technology, and its resources. Some will not. Before moving on, try your hand at writing goal and objectives statements. These will be helpful to you when we go over the anatomy of a proposal in the next chapter.

EXERCISE 7.1
WRITING STATEMENTS OF GOALS AND
OBJECTIVE

(1) Start off with a brief description (a paragraph or less) of a current or anticipated problem or a desired state of affairs.

(2) Identify one goal from that description. If you began with the description of a problem, the goal can be phrased as the absence of that problem or its converse. If you began with a normative statement, the goal will be implicit within it. Write the goal in a single sentence.

Does the goal speak to populations, services, or management? Should it speak to some that are? Are different goal statements needed for each, or are some not relevant to the problem you wish to deal with or the programs you are beginning to think about? Make whatever adjustments may be needed.

Do you think it clearly spells out the direction or aim of the activities that will have to be undertaken to accomplish the goal? Is it an energizing statement? Will it serve to legitimate subsequent efforts? If not, make whatever adjustment are needed.

(3) Now derive the performance objectives from the goal statement. Remember that the objective can be phrased in terms of operations, activities, impact, or all three. They should be specific enough to serve as the basis for monitoring or evaluating operations, activities and outcomes; that is, they should be measurable and time specific.

ASSESSING YOUR POSITION AMONG RELEVANT PUBLICS

The achievement of any of your objectives will depend on the extent to which (1) resources will be available from suppliers, (2) both your organization and the goals it has established for a particular program are considered legitimate, (3) other provider organizations are willing to cooperate with yours, and (4) consumer publics are ready to participate in the program established to reach those objectives.

Suppliers are those organizations, groups, and individuals that provide an organization with the resources necessary to produce its product, give its services, or maintain itself. A state agency, for example, might be the conduit through which the local agency receives funds for its services to the aging. A Community Mental Health Board or a United Fund might be an alternative or additional supplier of funds. A local volunteer bureau might be the supplier of supplementary manpower. A nearby university might provide the local agency with the necessary expertise to assess a need, evaluate a program, or provide a new service.

Most institutional providers are responsible to boards of directors, legislative bodies, governmental agencies, or other bodies under whose auspices they operate. At the local level an agency's board of directors may provide it with both auspices and legitimacy. In addition, some agencies are regulated by local, state, or national bodies. For example, family service agencies are licensed and legitimated through voluntary affiliation with the Family Service Association of America, which also imposes certain regulatory constraints on its member agencies. Many other voluntary agencies, such as Jewish Community Centers. YMCAs, and settlement houses, are also responsible to boards of directors or other sponsoring groups. It is not unusual for them to be further regulated by local health and welfare councils. All of these bodies provide the agency with additional legitimacy to the extent that they too are considered legitimate enterprises.

In any situation in which there is a scarcity of resources, there is also likely to be competition for those resources. A limited supply of volunteers or of funds for services to the developmentally disabled may cause competition among service providers. Conversely, when services are in abundant supply and there is insufficient demand, agencies may compete for consumers. For example, in periods of oversupply and underdemand, recreation agencies compete for participants, or nursing homes for patients. Some "voc rehab" agencies have been known to compete for trainees with the greatest potential for rehabilitation and placement. At times, agencies compete for a particular clientele with certain attributes based on racial, ethnic, or socioeconomic characteristics.

These very same organizations are also potential collaborators. Agencies that receive funds from the same source (the United Way or the state Mental Health Department, for example), also are likely to collaborate on the referral of clients, exchange of staff expertise, joint use of facilities, and so on.

Generally, people needing service are defined as an agency's actual or potential consumers. These *direct* recipients of an agency's service or product might be clients in a welfare agency, patients in a nursing home or hospital, users of a bus service for the handicapped, members of a Golden Age Club, or participants in a city recreation department's summer crafts program. In some cases one agency is the consumer and subsequently the distributor of another agency's services. An agency that receives technical assistance from a welfare council, or volunteers from a volunteer bureau, is the consumer of another's services. It redistributes those services to a user population.

In Chapter 3 through 6 you worked on a number of exercises related to assessment of suppliers of funds. In Chapter 2 you reviewed a wide variety of potential linking mechanisms aimed at increasing collaboration with the agencies. In Exercise 7.2 you will have the opportunity to identify various consumer publics according to their functional, geographic, demographic, and psychographic characteristics. We will take these one at a time. Typically, when program planners examine their actual and potential consumer populations, they focus on a particular presenting problem, its incidence, and its severity.

This is what might be called the *functional* concerns, those identified as needs or related to particular services that the agency currently provides or hopes to be able to provide. These functional concerns are generally divided into health, mental health, employment, and other areas. Sometimes they are organized by age group: child welfare, aging, and youth concerns. At times concerns are organized by problems such as developmental disabilities or neighborhood decay. Within each of those areas and arenas, more specific subareas may be identified. Thus, concern with developmental disabilities might be focused only on families whose children suffer from Down's syndrome.

Another way of targeting populations to be served is by specifying the *geographic* or catchment area from which clients may be drawn or within which they will be served. These need not be coterminous. For example, a college may draw from a statewide applicant pool, but provide its services only on one home campus and several satellite stations. *Demographic* characteristics may further limit or pinpoint the populations to be served by age, test scores, gender, cultural or ethnic group, economic status, and so on. Finally, potential consumers can be segmented according to *psychographic* characteristics, such as willingness to make a commitment to providing as well as receiving service, acceptance of the service agency's philosophy of family life, and so on.

In Exercise 7.2 you will have an opportunity to use them again for segmenting actual and potential consumer populations. You can also use the same concepts for reexamining funders, auspice providers, and collaborating service agencies. All four publics may have to agree on the appropriateness of the clients you choose to serve if they are to provide you with the resources, legitimacy, and complementary services necessary to make your agency programs go.

EXERCISE 7.2
ASSESSING YOUR CLIENT POPULATIONS

Using the Assessment Form for Identifying Consumer Characteristics, or a similar form of your own design, follow the instructions below.

(1) Start by identifying the characteristics of your current consumer population. Be as specific as possible. For example, if you treat people with health problems, do not use the term *health* to describe the functional arena. Be more specific (e.g., renal diseases, hypertension, and so on).
Be just as specific for geographic, demographic, and psychographic characteristics.

(2) Now spell out the characteristics of the potential pool of consumers for the program or project you have in mind. This may be different, similar, broader, or narrower than the population currently being served. Be sure to exclude the non-market, those populations that you will not be interested in attracting or which you would not wish to attract.

(3) Finally, spell out the desired characteristics for the population you hope to serve with the new program or project. This will be a more narrow segment. It will include those persons and groups that are to be the primary target of intervention.

(4) How do the characteristics under each of the columns differ? What would you have to do to attract the population with the desired characteristics? Are persons with these characteristics available from the potential consumer pool in sufficient numbers to make it possible to conduct the service with the resources currently or potentially available? Do you anticipate that demand will be over full, full, too low, steady, or variable (perhaps by season)?

(5) Consider examining the consumer characteristics of other agencies with which your organization may be linked in some way. How do these characteristics fit those that funders or auspice providers may be interested in financing or legitimating?

Sketch out your preliminary thoughts on these issues.

CARVING OUT AN APPROPRIATE *NICHE* IN THE MARKET

5.

It is not sufficient to decide who your consumers will be, who will supply the necessary resources, or who will cooperate with your organization in providing the planned-for services. Unless others agree that your organization has a legitmate claim over a particular domain, the organization is not likely to be successful in carving out a special niche of its own. There will have to be agreement that your organization has the capacity to provide needed services, that those services are in fact needed and are likely to produce desired results, that the consumers you intend to serve are deserving and in need, and that your organization is a worthy and dependable partner in the delivery of services. Incidentally, the same considerations apply when you try to carve out a niche for a particular program or project in your own organization.

That consensus is most likely to be reached if there are no competing claims for domain, and if the organization has a proven track record for accomplishing what it sets out to do. But what if there is competition? What if your organization has a poor track record, or perhaps no track record at all because it is new on the scene or new to the particular service you intend to provide? And what if the key funding, legitimating, collaborating, or consumer publics are unaware of your organization and what it hopes to do?

Unfortunately, there are no uniform answers to these questions. What you can or cannot do is often defined by others. Your *niche*, the place you occupy in relation to various publics, may be the result of

Exercise 7.2

ASSESSMENT FORM FOR IDENTIFYING CONSUMER CHARACTERISTICS

Segmentation Variable	Current Clients	Potential Client Pool	Desired Client Characteristics
Functional Area or Arena			
Geographic Area from Which Consumers Are/Can or Should Be Drawn			
Demographic Characteristics			
Psychographic Characteristics			

environmental factors more than anything that the organization does on its own behalf. Nevertheless, you can increase your organization's claim to a particular niche or turf through a number of tactics. These include (1) fact finding and dissemination, (2) promotions, (3) trade-offs, and (4) getting the necessary endorsements.

Fact finding is another way of describing the process of problem specification we discussed earlier. You will have to document the existence of a problem, its severity, and the consequences of both action and inaction by your organization for those populations in need and for those who may be indirectly affected by the problem. You will also have to make certain that those publics who need to have access to that information or who may need sensitization to it are informed. The same holds true if you are making a normative approach. In this case you will have to document the desirability of the state of affairs you hope to promote and to show how it differs in a positive way from the current situation.

That is what *promotion* is all about. Throughout the book, we have described a number of promotional approaches. These included use of the print media, radio, and television; outreach; personal contacts; direct appeals; or education through personal appearances, lectures, small group meetings and so on. What were the activities performed by the promoters of the hospice described in Chapter 2? Of the health organization that worked with firefighters discussed in Chapter 6? Of those persons working with the private sector in Chapter 5?

How can your organization get its message across through the daily newspapers, monthly or weekly neighborhood or community journals, and civic group and industrial newsletters? Has its programs or the needs of targeted populations been discussed on the radio or television? Are your staff, board members, and organized clients involved in making public appearances before community groups, the local city council, targeted churches, and service clubs? Has word of mouth been used effectively? Are fund-raising campaigns used to heighten public awareness and commitment to action?

Trade-offs refer to the process of give-and-take in which one party agrees to modify its demands or its aspirations in response to those of another party. It may also require that the organization give something up in return for a desired resource or agreement. We are speaking here of the process of exchange in which two or more parties agree to collaborate because of the shared expectation that collaboration will net benefits that outweigh the costs incurred, or that outweigh the consequences of nonaccommodation. The parties need not benefit equally. It is only necessary that they all perceive the exchange to have some payoff now or in the future. Thus, in order to induce another agency to refer its clients, you may have to modify your agency's procedures or agree to provide the other agency with something it needs in return. Receipt of an award from a government or foundation funding source may require that your organization modify its program goals somewhat in order to accommodate to the funder's priorities or funding limitations. Inducing clients to seek service from your agency may require that you relocate some of those services to make them more accessible.

Endorsements are of central importance if the reputation or capability of your organization is in doubt or if the facts of the case — the problem that needs addressing or the severity of the problem and its possible consequences — are not fully understood or agreed upon. Endorsements might be made by other funding sources that have been satisfied with your organization's performance, by collaborating service providers that testify to their willingness to cooperate on a given project, by current or former consumers who testify to either the problem or to the appropriateness of your agency's intervention plan. From where else might endorsements come? To what extent is the participation of key influentials on your agency's board, on a planning group, or in a fund-raising campaign implicit endorsements? How can you capitalize on their involvement? Which of these individuals, groups, or organizations might introduce you to a potential funder or consumer group?

GETTING THE *INFORMATION* YOU NEED IN ORDER TO ACT

By now you may feel you have enough information to take action. You have, after all, checked out your *organization,* defined the problem or the desired state of affairs, identified the *resources* you will need and where they can be found, determined your *goals* and specified your operational objectives, *assessed* your position among relevant publics, determined the *niche* you wish to carve out for the organization or the project you have in mind. What you have not done is seek out *information* on other programs and projects that may be similar to yours and upon which you might pattern your intervention efforts.

For any intervention efforts, there are generally more alternatives than one. For example, if the objectives have to do with providing health information, your agency might consider meeting the need through a study course, home visits, a radio program, a newspaper column, a clinic, or a public lecture series.

All possibilities should be investigated, and the one most feasible for achieving the projected objectives in the local situation should be selected. The agency must be prepared to give sound reasons for whatever choice it makes.

Funders often know about projects similar to yours. Federal agencies, for example, often publish abstracts or summaries of recently funded projects. The Rehabilitation Services Administration sends one-page abstracts on the projects it funded in the previous year along with an application kit for currently available grants. The Community Mental Health Centers Branch at the National Institute of Mental Health periodically abstracts descriptions of projects it has funded and publishes them in a summary book. The National Clearing House on Aging is funded by the Administration on Aging to disseminate information on selected projects that have been identified in each state as being worthy of emulation. The "Children's Bureau" has funded a network of national and regional centers to promote innovation in child welfare.

A good place to get additional information is in the professional literature: the journals and periodicals published in your field. National associations conduct local, state, regional and national meetings at which presentations on innovative and successful projects are reported. Large foundations and companies in the private sector frequently publish reports on demonstration programs they have funded and which they feel should be duplicated, and which may accrue prestige to the funder. Local agencies often learn about projects in other localities by contacting the national organizations with which they are affiliated.

Project SHARE (located at 5600 Fishers Lane, Rockville, Maryland 20852) is a good source of information on community development and social action projects. It publishes monographs on practice, annotated bibliographies, and "fugitive" literature — reports on programs and projects that may appear only in the annual reports of the sponsoring organizations.

Why reinvent the wheel if you can learn from someone else's experience? Why not build on that experience, improve on it, modify it to achieve your particular objectives, or tailor it to your local circumstances.

ZERO IN ON PROGRAMS AND ACTIVITIES   7.

You are now ready to *zero* in on possible programs and the activities they comprise. An approach I have found useful in exploring all the alternatives is the use of a "branching tree" approach. It actually begins by spreading out rather than zeroing in. The branching tree is a form of idea inventory or brainstorming on paper.

It is a relatively simple procedure, although it may take quite some time to carry out. Like other rational models, it is best used to explore all of the possibilities before you decide what to do and how. It starts with problem definition, then breaks down each general problem into its component parts. For each subproblem, a goal is selected, and this goal is used to generate operational objectives. There may be a number of alternative interventions (e.g., service programs) that can be used to achieve a given objective. Sometimes, several interventions in tandem may be necessary. Once you have identified these alternatives, the final step is to identify the components of each intervention (i.e., what has to be done or put into place in order for it to come off). The process works somewhat as shown in Figure 7.1.

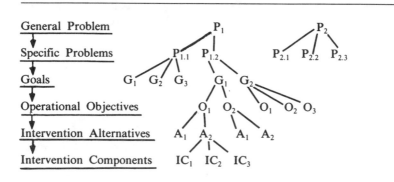

Figure 7.1 The Branching Tree Process

In looking over the example, you will find that the longest branch is $P_1 - P_{1.2}G_1O_1 - A_2 - IC_1 + IC_2 + IC_3$. Had all the branches, starting with P_1 and P_2, been carried out fully, we would have ended with several hundred intervention approaches. You will probably need a chalkboard or newsprint to complete all the branches. Use Exercise 7.3 as your guide. It includes instructions as well as an example.

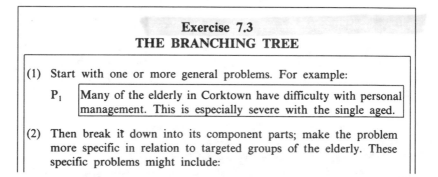

Exercise 7.3
THE BRANCHING TREE

(1) Start with one or more general problems. For example:

P_1 | Many of the elderly in Corktown have difficulty with personal management. This is especially severe with the single aged.

(2) Then break it down into its component parts; make the problem more specific in relation to targeted groups of the elderly. These specific problems might include:

$P_{1.1}$ | Nutritional Deficiencies

$P_{1.2}$ | Poor management of personal budgets.

$P_{1.3}$ | Inability to do basic housekeeping or to perform household repairs.

$P_{1.4}$ | Difficulty in getting about for purposes of shopping or getting to service providers.

(3) Use these more specific problems to establish your goals. For example, "nutritional deficiencies" might result in your determining that:

G_1 | Older people, particularly those isolated in rural areas, will be fed nutritiously.

(4) Now it is time to define your operational objectives.* The following might be included:

O_1 | Eighty percent of the persons in the target area will receive information about diets and how they can manage nutritious eating programs on a limited budget.

O_2 | Prepared foods, at an affordable cost will be available close to home to 500 people by the end of the second year of the project's operation.

(5) How might these objectives be reached? Let us take the second objective. Service alternatives might include:

A_1 | Meals-on-Wheels Home Delivery.

A_2 | Congregate meal sites at local schools and churches.

A_3 | Cooperative cooking programs in conjunction with the Coop Food Buying program.

(6) Each of these requires a number of service components. The meals-on-wheels alternative, for example, might require:

IC_1 | Outreach and case finding of potential elderly participants.

IC_2 | Sites at which food can be prepared.

IC_3 | A nutritionist who can design menus and supervise meal preparation.

IC_4 | Volunteers for food preparation and transportation to homes.

SOURCE: Adapted from an approach developed by Yeheskel Hasenfeld.
* Review earlier discussion of operations, activity, and outcome objectives.

Exercise 7.3
Schematic Guide for Branching Tree Program Design
Using the sample track as a guide, design your own branching tree specifying all the choices possible. Note that space limitations do not permit tracking from more than one antecedent on each component or branch below.

KEY

P_1	General Problem	O_1	Operational Objective
$P_{1.1}$	Specific Problem	A_1	Intervention Alternative
G_1	Goal	IC_1	Intervention Component

If you completed the exercise, you may have generated six or seven hundred alternative program or intervention components. How will you choose between them? The following judgment criteria may be useful: (1) frequently of appearance, (2) feasibility, (3) complementarity with organizational mission, (4) likelihood of contributing to objectives without negative side effects or consequences, (5) acceptability to various publics; and (6) compatibility. Let us take one at a time.

Certain program *components* tend to *appear frequently* at the ends of different branches. On one tree, for example, one might find "counseling," "outreach," "transportation," "volunteer training," or "support groups" appearing many times. Any one of these components may appear at the ends of branches that have different origins. You might discover that volunteer training contributes to the conduct of several interventions, to the achievement of several objectives, perhaps even to the accomplishment of several goals and to the resolution of more than one problem. The training of volunteers will not be the only thing that needs doing, but it may contribute to the accomplishment of many objectives.

Feasibility refers to the likelihood that a particular program component can be put in place. How available are the needed resources of money and credit, facilities, trained or committed staff, political influence, organizational and personal time and energy, and legitimacy?

Are the program components you have tentatively selected compatible with the organization's history and sense of *mission?* Or are they such wide departures from the norm that they are likely either to generate resistance or move the organization into new and untried paths for which it may not be ready? Are they functional for the organization; that is, will they contribute to achievement of its program missions; its staff and board aspirations; its need for resources and community support?

Some program components, although rated high on feasibility and frequency of appearance, may nonetheless contribute little to the achievement of *program goals* that are considered paramount. In such cases, they may divert the organization from investing its energies and other resources where they count the most. Even those that do contribute directly to the achievement of priority goals, may lead to undesired side effects or have unanticipated consequences. For example, a one-time food distribution effort may generate such high demand, that the agency may find itself permanently in the food business although that was never its intention. A volunteer program once established, may place demands on the paid professional staff for support and ongoing training to such a degree that little time is left for them to do what they prefer — working directly with clients.

There is also the question of *acceptability*. Are the program components acceptable to various key publics; agency funders; clients; board members? If not, are they likely to generate conflict, or just indifference? Can you live with the indifference; deal with the conflict? Are other components so clearly acceptable that they will overcome disagreements over those that are not?

Finally, there is the question of the compatibility of one component to another. For example, in the Detroit freeway case, establishing a bus lane that reduces the lanes accessible to cars might be incompatible with widening or increasing the number of exit ramps. Clearly, some goals and some objectives may have to be put aside if others are to be adopted.

Figure 7.2 will be helpful in making decisions about intervention components. For example, on completion of the branching tree, should you find a component rarely present, and judge it to be unfeasible and in any case not complementary to the organization's missions, you might eliminate it from consideration. If an item is rated high on all or almost all the variables, you might consider it seriously. When an item scores high on some variables, and none or minimal on others, more careful examination will be necessary. For example, an outreach program aimed at teen substance abusers may be right on target (high) on contributions to objectives and on feasibility. But it may be low on complementarity and it may be low on acceptability to some of the organization's constituencies. What to do? At this point there is no formula. Personal value judgments, staff and board preferences, the availability of funds and other resources; all these may lead to a go or no go decision.

ESTABLISH AN ACTION PLAN FOR ACHIEVING YOUR OBJECTIVES

You are almost home free; ready to design your proposal or start your action program. At this point all that is required is to decide who is to do what and by what time. Mary Hall, who has written an excellent guide to proposal writing, suggests the following approach to designing a timetable for proposal development. The time frame and the activities and the persons involved may be different in your situation, but the approach she suggests is a useful one. Look over the Timetable in Exercise 7.4 and complete the final exercise of the chapter.

	1 Frequency of Appearance	2 Feasibility	3 Complementarity With Missions	4 Contribution to Objectives	5 Acceptability	6 Compatibility
High						
Somewhat						
Low or Minimal						

Figure 7.2 Program Component Decision-Making Guide

EXERCISE 7.4
DESIGNING A TIMETABLE

(1) Decide on who else should be involved in reviewing your program ideas, establishing an action plan, setting a fund-raising process in motion, writing a proposal, and so on. Write their names on a sheet of paper, and next to each, indicate the reason why they should be involved:
  ● access to resources
  ● key decision makers in the organization
  ● potential endorsers with key publics
  ● representatives of important interest groups or populations (e.g., women, minorities, middle managers, volunteers, other service providers with which collaborative exchanges will be necessary)
  ● expertise in planning, proposal writing, budgeting, and so on.
(2) How will you invite them? What inducements will you use: Their interest in the project or the agency? the prestige of being involved? some other trade-off?
Good luck!

Exercise 7.4
TIMETABLE FOR PROPOSAL DEVELOPMENT

MONTH	ACTIVITY
March	Idea identified. Preliminary discussions held with colleagues in local agency to determine their interest; contact made with colleagues in other communities or states to determine the regional or national significance of the idea. Preliminary discussion held with agency administrators.
April	Needs assessment instituted. Inquiries submitted to national information systems [see Chapter 2] to determine if similar idea has already been tried, to get names of communities or agencies with related experience and to identify related research. Statistical data collected to support statement of need.
May	Various approaches to implement idea discussed. Best approach chosen after contacts made with other local agencies, state agencies, etc. Approval to proceed with development of project obtained from administrators. Project director or program developer selected and other staff to be involved in proposal preparation. First draft of ideas in project form developed and discussed with agency administrators, potential population to be served, and other groups necessary to local support.
June	Potential funding sources identified and preliminary outline sent to determine their interest in the project and to acquire necessary application information [see Chapter 3].
July	Project idea modified by input received during previous months. Another inquiry to potential funding sources may be warrented. Second draft completed and circulated for review to agency administrators and any local or state group involved in a clearance procedure.
August	Funding source chosen. Final draft prepared based on source's forms or requirements. Official clearance received from local administrators. Review and clearance sought as necessary from any local or state agencies.
September	Proposal submitted to funding source. Receipt card with processing number received in return.
December to February	Approval or rejection received. In either case comments of reviewers should be sought.
March	Authorization for expenditure received.

April	Recruitment of personnel. Modifications started on facilities, if necessary.
May-June	Plans developed for staff training. Materials prepared.
July	Personnel salaried and project started. Staff training initiated. Detailed management plan outlined. Assignments and responsibilities clarified.
October	Refunding application prepared and submitted.

SOURCE: Mary Hall, *Developing Skills in Proposal Writing*. Eugene: University of Oregon Continuing Education Publications, 1979.

REVIEW

We have just worked our way through the process of GETTING ORGANIZED. Eight sets of activities were described. These are part of the planning process that any organization must go through in program design and resource development. We began be examining (1) the *organization* that is to sponsor or develop the program and identifying potential sources of resistance and support. We then went on to (2) to identify the *resources* necessary to get something done, and their sources of supply. We (3) defined current or anticipated problems, established an image of a desirable state of affairs, determined the *goals* to be achieved and specified the operational objectives that flow from those goals.

We went on to (4) *assess* the various consumers, legitmators, resource suppliers and potential partners in the enterprise being considered. We (5) carved out a *niche* for the organization or for the project within it. We (6) examined a variety of sources of *information* on other projects or programs from which we might learn so as to adapt their experiences to our own settings. We (7) used a branching tree exercise to examine all the possible alternatives and *zeroed in* on those that seemed most do-able under the circumstances. Finally, we (8) *established* an action plan for setting the process in motion.

SUGGESTIONS FOR FURTHER READING

There are a number of sources for additional information on program planning and design. You are probably already familiar with some. The following list will suggest additional approaches and build on those suggested in this chapter.

Blakely, E. J. "Goal setting for community development — case of Yuba City, California." *Rural Sociality* 44 (2), 1979, 434-436.

Brody, Ralph. *Problem Solving: Concepts and Methods for Community Organization*. New York: Human Sciences Press, 1982.

Craig, Dorothy. *A Hip Pocket Guide to Planning and Evaluation.* Austin, TX: Learning Concepts Publications, 1976.

Dale, D., & Mitigui, N. *Planning for a Change.* Amherst, MA: Citizen Involvement Training Project, 1978.

Glidewell, John C. *Choice Points.* Cambridge: MIT Press, 1976.

Kilmann, R., Pondy, L. R., & Slevin, D. P., (Eds.). *The Management of Organization Design: Strategies and Implementation.* New York: North-Holland, 1976.

Lauffer, Armand. *Assessment Tools: For Practitioners, Managers and Trainers.* Beverly Hills, CA: Sage, 1982.

——— *Getting the Resources You Need.* Beverly Hills, CA: Sage, 1982.

——— *Social Planning at the Community Level.* Englewood Cliffs, NJ: Prentice-Hall, 1978.

——— *Strategic Marketing* (tent). New York: Free Press, (forthcoming).

Lippitt, R., Watson, J., and Westley, B. *The Dynamics of Planned Change.* New York: Harcourt Brace, 1958.

Magee, John. "Decision trees for decision making." *Harvard Business Review,* July-August 1964, 126-28.

Mager, Robert. *Goal Analysis.* Belmont, CA: Fearon Publishers, 1972.

Neuber, Keith et al. *Needs Assessment: A Model for Community Planning.* Beverly Hills, CA: Sage, 1981.

Rein, Martin & Morris, Robert. "Goals, structures and strategies for community change," in Ralph Kramer and Harry Specht (Eds.), *Readings in Communities Organization Practice.* Englewood Cliffs, NJ: Prentice-Hall, 1983.

Resnick, Hyman & Patti, Rino. (Eds.). *Change from Within: Humanizing Social Welfare Organizations.* Philadelphia: Temple University Press, 1980.

Young, R. C. "Goals and goal setting." *Journal of the American Institute of Planners,* March 1966, 32, 76-85.

Zander, Alvin. "Resistance to change: Its analysis and prevention," in Warren G. Bennis, Kenneth D. Benne, & Robert Chin (Eds.), *The Planning of Change: Readings in Applied Behavioral Science.* New York: Holt, Rinehart & Winston, 1962.

Chapter 8

WRITING THE PROJECT PROPOSAL
A Blueprint for Action

VIGNETTE 13: A PLAN FOR ACTION

*I represent the school of thought that espouses clarity and precise
statements of intentions in proposals. I do not view a proposal as a*
precursor *to a design or to a plan for action. A proposal should* be a plan
*for action. It should be written in operational terms. It should offer clear
and precise projections about strategies, activities, and schedules, end
results, and so on. If a project is intended to have a specific impact, that
impact should be detailed in the proposal. Impact should be measurable,
and the writer should indicate how it is to be measured.*

*The way I look at it, if funds are granted, planners should not then sit
back and ask themselves what to do next. The next step should be clear
from the proposal. I can't repeat too often that a proposal should be a
"plan for action." It's a deliberate, rational design for social intervention.*

*I've been around long enough to know many planners who regard proposal
writing with utter cynicism. "Give the funders what they want," they
figure, "and they'll give you what you want." While there may be some
validity to their position, I'm not willing to let this perspective govern my
actions. I never promise more than I know I can produce. I think I've
developed a reputation for integrity. We're not in the fast buck business.
We're in it for the long haul. Intent, integrity, and successful grantseeking
go hand in hand* [adapted from Armand Lauffer, *Grantsmanship,* first
edition. Beverly Hills, CA: Sage, 1977].

PUTTING IT DOWN ON PAPER

I could not agree more. In this chapter we will examine what goes
into successful proposals. It is not just what you put into a proposal,
however, or how you write it. The clarity and sincerity of the intent will
also be evaluated against the funder's own interests and priorities.
Proposals are statements of intent; they are intended to serve as a

beginning blueprint for action. If you have checked out your environment, identified the appropriate funding source or sources, examined your own organization's capability, and followed our other suggestions for "getting organized," you are ready to commit the proposal to paper. There is, of course, no perfect pattern to recommend for all grant applications. If I were to suggest any single hard-and-fast rule, it is this: Follow exactly whatever instructions are spelled out by the prospective funder.

Each funding source will have its own special requirements. In some cases, instructions on format and length will be quite detailed. In other cases the funder will permit you considerable latitude. This will not only vary with different funders, but with the kinds of projects they are likely to support. For example, research proposals are likely to require a significant review of the literature, a rigorous methodology section, and some attention paid to the significance of this particular project in light of previous findings or the problem examined.

Those oriented toward the provision of services will require documentation on the needs of those to be served or problems to be addressed. You may have to justify your proposal in terms of the lack of other available or efficient services, the anticipated impact of your project, and the potential for its replication elsewhere. If you are designing a training proposal, you will probably be asked to show the connections between training and service delivery and may be required to justify your project in terms of reduction in costs or increase in effectiveness of service programs.

THE ANATOMY OF A PROPOSAL

Keeping these differences in mind, we think it is nevertheless possible to examine the anatomy of a typical proposal. Generally it includes the following components:

1. the title and cover pages,
2. the project narrative,
3. the capacities of your agency or organization,
4. the budget,
5. an appendix.

Before examining each of these components, I want to share a few suggestions with you. First, try to keep your narrative down to a reasonable length. Reviewers have a hard time dealing with more than fifteen pages and usually prefer a document that is no more than twelve pages long. Some foundations and businesses may limit you to five or six pages. This may not give you sufficient space to detail the scope of the problem you are addressing, to describe your organization's capacity, or to properly explain your budget. That's what the appendix is for.

If the reviewer wants more information, refer him or her to the appendix. Here, you can be as detailed as you wish. I often set off the appendix so as not to overwhelm the reader. For example, I use white for the cover pages, the narrative, and the information about the organization and budget, but I find it useful to duplicate the appendix in a different color. This is especially true when the appendix is three or four times as thick as the rest of the document. Don't minimize the problems that the reviewer may have in going over your proposal. The easier you make it, the more attention will be paid to the substance of your proposal rather than its form.

For that reason, I recommend you use simple, concise language, presenting the facts of the case in a straightforward manner. Avoid the eloquence of professional jargon. Many of the best administrators and program developers I know have writing hangups. If you find yourself in this position, get some help. You don't have to go to a professional writer. You may need an editor to go over your first draft. Or you may need someone to put it down on paper the first time around. That won't absolve you of the hard work of making detailed notes for each component. Effective collaboration on any writing project takes some time to develop. The first joint writing effort may be a bit rough or may take longer than you anticipate. Give yourself enough time. It will pay off in the final document.

PREPARING THE COVER AND TITLE PAGES

Most governmental funding agencies include forms for the title page or pages. Make certain you leave none of the required information incomplete. Follow the instructions given, to the letter. Proposals with incomplete title pages may not be accepted.

If no standard form is required, include the following information on the title page of your own design:

1. title of the project,
2. name and address of your agency or organization,
3. submitted to (name of funding source),
4. proposed project dates,
5. the amount of money requested for this fiscal year and over the life of the project,
6. date of submission,

7. the name and signature of the project director and/or official who will
    be legally responsible for the project,
8. a one-paragraph abstract.

Your cover page or pages may also differ from the others in color or
weight of paper. But they should not be elaborate or slick. Even when
an abstract is not required by the funding agency, it is a good idea to
include one. The abstract can be used by the reviewer to get a quick
overview of what the proposal is all about. It can be used by the funder
to code the types or nature of projects under consideration and for
dissemination of information about projects reviewed or funded.

Typically, an abstract is no longer than two hundred words. It
summarizes the objectives and significance of the project, the procedures to be followed in carrying it out, and the plans for evaluating the
results or making the results available to others. Facts given elsewhere
on the title page need not be repeated in the abstract unless specifically
required by the funder.

THE PROJECT NARRATIVE

The narrative should include all or most of the following information: (1) need or problem addressed; (2) objectives to be reached; (3)
specification of the problem; (4) populations to be served, or systems to
be targeted; (5) alternative approaches to dealing with the problem or
serving the population; (6) procedures to be followed; (7) schedule or
timetable; (8) administration and staffing; (9) evaluation; (10) dissemination and special features; and (11) continuation.

It is not unusual for the funder to request this information in a
different order. For example, most federal agencies require information
about your organization to appear first in the narrative. The schedule or
timetable is often a separate item appearing after the narrative or
somewhere between the narrative and the budget or appendixes.
Research proposals may follow a different format. So may training
proposals. Proposals for capital expenditures certainly will. A number
of the suggested categories can be collapsed. Remember to follow the
instructions given by the funding source. The funder may not need all
this information. Alternatively, the funder may have other questions it
wants addressed.

The instructions that follow presume you are working on an action
or service delivery proposal. I have found it useful to draw up a brief
statement of the problem or need (about a half-page) and to locate it at
the start of the narrative. Answer the following questions:

What   is the situation that concerns the planner?
        makes this a problem?

Who   is directly affected?
is indirectly affected?

Where is the problem located with reference to this program?

Follow this up with a statement of the goals and objectives to be reached. These might also be written to take no more than a half-page. The goals and objectives statement should be in vivid contrast to the statement of the problem. Review the discussion of goals and objectives and your completed exercise material in Chapter 7. Remember that while goals are stated in general terms, objectives are stated in performance terms. They specify:

- what is to be done (operations or activities), and/or the outcome expected;
- and within what time frame.

Some objectives also include the

- conditions under which performance is to take place, or the
- criteria by which you will know whether or not the objective(s) has (have) been reached.

If there are too many objectives to include in this brief section, consider writing only the goal statement and relocate the objectives in the section on approaches to be followed.

Wherever it appears, a properly designed statement of objectives will do several things for you. It will establish the criteria against which your project can be evaluated. It will provide you with a base from which you will design your intervention approaches, your training strategy, or your research methods. You may now want to go back to specification of the problem you outlined earlier. Your other statement may be too brief to provide an adequate basis for action. This section should include both conceptual and empirical material.

On the empirical side, you should describe the problem as concretely as possible. Determine whether the focus of attention is to be on (1) populations, groups, and individuals (e.g., skill, knowledge, and attitudes); (2) services (e.g., availability, accessibility, effectiveness, efficiency, and accountability); or (3) management (e.g., internal — productivity, relationship, authority, innovation, or external — continuity and comprehensiveness).

Don't let your knowledge run away with you. Include only information on those aspects of the problem or need that you will be addressing in your project. Everything else is extraneous. If you include it, the reviewer will wonder why your project does not address a broader need or problem. You may refer to a preliminary study you have conducted or to other available data found in census reports, surveys, or agency reports. If these data are extensive, refer to them in the narrative, but locate the bulk of the information in the appendix.

Information is often trivial unless it is accompanied by some conceptualization or explanation. You may wish to explain how you perceive the cause of the problem and the conditions that accompany the problem. There are many ways to do this. I've never found a grants writer as eloquent in describing problem conceptualization as the person in Vignette 14.

VIGNETTE 14: USING CONCEPTS

I draw on the literature to put the problem in a more conceptual framework. It's not that I think there are many theories of causation in the social sciences leading directly to intervention strategies. But I do think that isolated facts are meaningless. They have to be ordered through some concepts, or else one's rationale for action stands on very tenuous grounds.

What I do is search the literature for concepts that help me to understand the problem. If my concern is with the alienation of older people, I'll go through the literature on alienation and identity to find some appropriate intervention strategy. If my concern is with powerlessness and lack of participation, I'll look for concepts to help me understand participatory action better.

There are times when I just don't know where to look in the literature. I may ask a colleague or a friend who is familiar with the problem. Or I may just fall back on a sort of trick I've developed that helps me get alternative insights into the causes of a problem. I borrowed it from a sociologist friend of mine. I make a "2 x 2" table.

Suppose I'm concerned with getting more elderly people to take advantage of a particular service agency's program. I might begin by jotting down on one piece of paper all the reasons why older people might not be taking advantage of the program. Is it because they don't know of its existence? Is it because the agency is located inconveniently or the hours make it impossible for potential clients to take advantage of the service? Do clients feel the agency staff is condescending or unresponsive to their interests? Do they distrust that agency or the kind of service it gives because of previous experience? Are the costs — financial or psychic — too great? Then I make a similar inventory of possible reasons that the agency is not able to serve that particular population. Is it because agency staff don't understand the needs of older people or of a particular ethnic minority among the aged? Is the technology they're using inappropriate to this population? Are there insufficient numbers of staff people available?

Next I try to match one of the problems on the agency side with one of the problems on the consumer or client side. I'll draw up a 2 x 2 table:

Client's Mistrust or Fear of

Agency's Technology

		+ (No Fear)	- (Fear)
	+	(1)	(2)
	(Appropriate)	++	+-
	(3)	(4)	
	(Not Appropriate)	-+	--

If, on analysis, I find that the agency's technology is appropriate and the clients neither mistrust nor fear it, as indicated in Box 1, above, then I know that's not the reason they're not making use of the service. On the other hand, the technology may be appropriate but the clients may fear it (Box 2). In this case, I know that part of the solution is related to consumer education or more effective outreach by the agency. What if the facts show that there is no consumer anxiety, but the agency's services are nevertheless inappropriate (Box 3)? In this case, the appropriate action might be to get consumers to help educate the agency staff about what a particular client group really needs, or to put some pressure on that agency to change its procedures. It may also be important to create some staff training or development activities. But what if the agency's technology is bad and clients mistrust the agency (Box 4)? Some planners make the mistake of trying to move directly from Box 4 to Box 1. That seems to me to be a giant step. It may be more appropriate to move from Box 4 to Box 2 and then to Box 1.

Generally, I try to create the same 2 x 2 boxes for every logical combination of service blockages from both the agency perspective and the client perspective. When that's done, I suggest a strategy or set of strategies for dealing with the problem. I can now define the problem in operational terms. It's possible for me to list alternative intervention strategies and then select the best course of action. In my proposal, I give reasons for my selection. More than likely, the reasons will have to do with feasibility — that is, with what can be accomplished in view of available resources, support at the community level, the time available, and the political or sociological constraints limiting our possible interventions.

The grant writer has moved us to the next section of the narrative: that which examines alternative intervention approaches and describes which ones are to be pursued. Before we move on as well, let us make sure we have said all that needs saying about the populations to be served or targets of intervention. In designing a new service delivery program, for example, your objective may have specified that you want to serve the elderly in a low-income neighborhood. Which elderly? Where are they located? How many are there? What are their specific characteristics, and how do these differ from the general population or from the elderly in other communities? Segment the population according to geography, function, demography, and psychography.

Some proposals will be aimed at effecting changes in target populations as well as in target organizations. For example, your projected intervention may be targeted on foster care workers and supervisors whose knowledge, attitudes, or skills require changing. It may also target the agency itself, its procedures, its politicies, and its patterns of resource allocation. What changes in each are required so that changes in one are not cancelled out by lack of change in the other?

Let's turn our attention now to the selection of an appropriate intervention approach or approaches from among several alternatives. These approaches may be based on your conceptualization of the problem. They may also come from an "idea inventory" you participated in with others, perhaps using the "branching tree" technique discussed in Chapter 7. The approach selected may also be drawn from your knowledge of how other agencies or projects have dealt with the problem. If you are replicating something that has been done elsewhere, or if it is somewhat different, indicate *why* and *how*. Your selection from among alternative approaches may be based on one or more of the following factors: the way you have conceptualized the problem; cost; the capacity of your agency and your staff; the novelty of your approach; your assessment of its effectiveness; the probability that it can be institutionalized within your organization; and/or the likelihood that it can be replicated elsewhere.

The section on "Procedures" is sometimes referred to by funding agencies as "Program Implementation" or "Methodology." It should be prepared with great care. This is a place where you map out the specific techniques or approaches you will use for delivering the proposed service or conducting the research. You may include how the staff will be recruited and trained, the way in which service recipients will be engaged or served, and what, if any, follow-up steps are to be taken.

This is the place that often receives the greatest scrutiny by the reviewer or reviewing panel. Reviewers may think you have done a good job in describing and analyzing the problem and in specifying your objectives. But if they don't think that you know how to conduct research or training or how to manage a service project properly, they are not likely to fund the project.

It often helps to divide this section into subsections, particularly if you can group the project's tasks into specific categories. A training project, for example, might include consultation, the design and testing of training materials, the development of a curriculum plan, and the training of specified populations. The procedures used in each of these subsections should be described separately.

It sometimes makes sense to describe these activities chronologically. This is especially true when one activity or subtask must be accomplished before another begins.

The inclusion of a time chart in the proposal gives evidence of serious planning on the part of the applicant agency. In its simplest form, the chart might include a column for the target date or dates or for the months of the year. Another column might include the corresponding activities to be conducted during those periods. At the next level of complexity, you might want to draw up what is sometimes referred to as a Gantt chart.

A PERT chart or some other variation of the critical path method might be even more impressive, but might provide an information overload. In addition to its uses for impressing the funder with your capability, you might find the time chart helpful in planning your activity, anticipating those peak times in which resources such as manpower and facilities will be needed, and monitoring your progress once the project is under way.

The next section of your narrative focuses on the project's administrative location within the overall agency. In which department or subunit will it be lodged? To whom is the project director administratively and programmatically responsible? will the project have an advisory committee or a policy board? Is it to be made up of agency staff or staff from other agencies, of agency consumers, and/or of a panel of experts drawn from a local or national pool? How are the members of the advisory or policy group to be selected? What are their specific responsibilities to be? You will also need to spell out the internal administrative arrangements within the project, the lines of authority and supervision, and the management procedures to be used.

This is also a good place to describe the staffing of the project. You will want to give brief job descriptions for all the key professional staff. If you are to use consultants, indicate for what purposes and to what extent they will be involved in the project. If you know who the persons will be who will perform each of the staff roles (such as the project

Sample Gantt Chart

	1st Quarter	2nd Quarter	3rd Quarter	4th Quarter
Staff				
Recruitment and Selection	—			
Training	—	—		
Advising Committee				
Appointed	—			
Meetings	—	—	—	—
Assessment				
Instrument Designed	—			
Survey Conducted		—		
Report Issues			—	
Block Checks				
Organizations Activities	—	—		
Meetings		— —	— —	— —
Association Formed			—	
Conference				—
Evaluation				
Ongoing Monitoring	——	——	——	——
Evaluation Designed		—		
Evaluation Conducted			—	—
Report Issued				—

director, associate director, assistant director, administrative assistant, senior researcher), indicate their names. Discuss their specific qualifications briefly. This may include previous work done or their other supportive or complementary roles within your organization or agency. More detailed information on the staff should be located in the appendix. It might include either abbreviated or complete résumés on each professional staff person to be involved in some significant fashion.

There are several issues to consider in setting up the project's evaluation procedures. Both the project's operations and its outcomes should be evaluated.[1] The evaluation of outcomes relates directly to the objectives you established for the project. Did you accomplish what you set out to? Were you able to serve the number of people you anticipated at the planned level of service? Did the behavior of staff change in terms of increasing permanence for children? What were your measures of attitude change?

The second focus of evaluation is on the project itself and the procedures used. Did you follow your time line? Were intraagency supports adequate? Was staff orientation sufficient? If the original plan was not followed, on what basis were changes made? This aspect of evaluation should occur throughout the project. It will permit you to monitor your progress according to plan and to make shifts in procedures or even in objectives if circumstances warrant.

Finally, your evaluation should indicate the connections between the procedures followed and the project outcomes.

At this point, you will want to make some statements about special features, replication, or dissemination. What distinguishes this approach from others? How does it articulate with the interests of the funder or those of other publics? How can successes be replicated elsewhere? How will the results be reported? How can others be alerted not to make the same mistakes or repeat the same errors that your staff may commit? Consider the kinds of project report or reports that will be prepared. To whom will they be distributed? Will there be any publications? Will dissemination occur only locally through news items or TV documentaries? Will staff share their experiences with representatives of other agencies in your locale? At regional and national meetings of professional associations?

In many instances, funders provide money to initiate a new program or service on the assumption that the recipient agency intends to continue the program beyond the initial grant. Is the project to be absorbed within the ongoing operation of your organization? If new financial resources are needed, from where will they come? From outside sources such as fees for service or other grants? From reallocation of the agency's internal budget? Even when a commitment to continuation is not specifically required, it is often helpful if the proposal demonstrates the applicant's concern for the future. This is particularly true when the absence of continued funding might jeopardize the client population through sudden termination of services.

ABOUT YOUR AGENCY AND ITS CAPACITIES

Having made your case for the need or the importance of the problem to be addressed, the relevance of your objectives, and the feasibility of your intervention plan, you must now provide convincing evidence that your organization has the competence to conduct the project successfully. If your agency has a good track record of conducting training programs, of managing research of national significance, or of innovative service, describe that record. This is no place to be modest.

If you already have an established relationship with the population to be served and have demonstrated an ability to make proper use of community resources, review the history of those relationships and your use of resources. Extensive information might be lodged in the appendix. Letters of endorsement from prominent people who are well acquainted with the funding agency as well as with your program are sometimes of value. These also belong in the appendix.

Some experienced proposal writers prefer including information about the project staff in this section rather than in the program narrative as we have suggested. We hold no brief for one approach or another. Just remember to include detailed résumés in the appendix for the director and other key professionals who will be involved in the project.

THE BUDGET

The best-laid plans must now be translated into dollars. It is the grant-seeking process, after all, that motivated you to write the proposal in the first place. We've known some awfully good project designers and proposal writers who turn over the responsibility for budget preparation to others who may be better with figures. This is a mistake. Only those who are thoroughly familiar with the objectives of the project and the procedures that will be used to accomplish those objectives should make the decisions about how much money will be sought and for which categories of expenditure. You may want to involve people who are knowledgeable about costs, but you won't turn over the decision on how to allocate money and for what to people who are not programmatically knowledgeable or administratively responsible.

Most funding agencies have set procedures for the budget description section in the proposal. Forms may be provided for inclusion in the cover pages. Additional explanations and justifications, however, may be requested. In general, most funders require a line budget itemization. Line budgets reflect expenditures. They show exactly what money will be used for.

The construction of a line-item budget is detailed in the next chapter. It is compared with functional budgets — those known as performance and program budgets, which can be used to cost out major activity complexes and the achievement of program objectives. You might want to read that chapter before completing your project narrative. Some proposal writers use the budget as a planning document. They design it first, before completing the rest of the project design or committing it to paper.

If you have completed the other parts of a proposal, you know pretty much what should go into the appendix. Consider including greater specification of the problem and the needs being addressed; (2) a review of the literature or of other service programs similar to the one you have projected; (3) information on both the agency and staff involved, including résumés; (4) more fully spelled out time projections; (5) full budget justifications; (6) letters of endorsement; and any other items you feel are relevant but not important enough to appear in the narrative itself.

THE FINISHING TOUCHES

You are not finished yet. After all parts of the proposal are committed to paper, a few steps remain. The first of these is to have the entire document reviewed from at least three viewpoints. The writer must check detail by detail to make sure all aspects of the project have been covered. Another person familiar with the project and your agency should determine whether the plan is accurately described. And someone without previous knowledge of the project should be asked to make sure that every section of the proposal is understandable.

You may find this brief checklist helpful in your final review:

- Are the important points easily discovered in skimming the proposal?
- Has the applicant made a convincing case for a specific local need, outlined a realistic plan for meeting that need, and demonstrated that it is the agency best positioned to carry out the plan?
- Are the stated objectives clearly reflected in the sections on procedures, personnel, and budget?
- Does the proposal present an honest, factual picture of the applicant agency and of the resources and personnel available for the project? Are the "plus" factors emphasized, but without exaggeration?
- Is the presentation grammatical, clear, and conside, avoiding jargon, overblown phraseology, and unexplained abbreviations?
- Have all requirements of the funding agency been met?

THE LETTER PROPOSAL:
A SPECIAL CASE

Throughout the chapter we have been assuming that you will be writing a full-length proposal.

Under certain circumstances, however, it may be appropriate to write a letter proposal. This is sometimes all that is required (or even allowed) by some foundations, civic associations, or business companies. Letter proposals need not exceed two pages of perhaps six or seven paragraphs. The emphasis is generally on the problem to be addressed or the need of a consumer population. Letter proposals should be tailored to the expressed interests of the funding source. The Outline for a Letter Proposal is adapted from suggestions made by the Public Management Institute.

Outline for a Letter Proposal

First Paragraph	(1)	*Addressee* — the person requesting the proposal or the official contact person at the funding source, to the address of the funding source.
	(2)	*Introduction* — the reason for writing, and in particular, to this funding source. For example: "Robin Martenns suggested that our interests and those of the foundation are closely related. I am writing about . . . "
Second Paragraph	(3)	*The Problem of the Need* — in one or two sentences state the problem, the need, or the desired state of affairs your project addresses. Examples: "Last year 87 people committed suicide in Midtown and 430 attempts were reported. We think there may have been twice that many." Or, "Books don't reach children in the west end."
Third Paragraph	(4)	*Your Proposed Action* — an outline of the project in 4 to 6 short sentences presented as a solution to the problem or need just described; include the timetable.
Fourth Paragraph	(5)	*Benefits* — how clients or the community will benefit from the intervention directly and indirectly; who else cares.
	(6)	*Unique Features* — how this project differs from others, the sponsors of the project (i.e., who was involved or who cares), complementarity with the funding source's interests.
Fifth Paragraph	(7)	*Budget* — brief summary, perhaps broken down into broad performance or program expenditures.
	(8)	*The Amount Requested* — dollars sought for this year or for entire project period, and amounts to be donated from other sources.

EXERCISE 8.1
WRITING YOUR OWN PROPOSAL

(1) Decide whether you wish to work on a full length or a letter proposal. Go to your reading notes on Chapters 7 and 18, or reexamine the chapters themselves and the exercises you completed for Chapter 7.

(2) Write a proposal using the categories suggested under Anatomy of a Proposal, or the Outline of a Letter Proposal, suggested in this chapter; or follow a funder's guidelines. If you are writing a budget, follow the instructions in Chapter 9.

(3) Review the proposal using the funder's review criteria or those suggested in Chapter 10.

SUMMARY

Full-length proposals are generally divided into the following sections: (1) the title and cover pages, (2) the project narrative, (3) the organization's capacities to do the job, (4) the budget, and (5) the appendix. The narrative is further subdivided into problem description, goals and objectives, populations to be served, alternative approaches to dealing with the problem or serving the population, approach to be taken and procedures to be followed, timetable, administration and staffing; evaluation, dissemination and special features, and continuation. Letter proposals are abridged versions of the above.

NOTE

1 Review the discussions on the "focus of attention" and "types of objectives" in the section on Goals in Chapter 7.

SUGGESTIONS FOR FURTHER READING

Borden, Karl. *Dear Uncle, Please Send Money — A Guide for Proposal Writers.* Pocatello, ID: Auger Associates, 1978.

Citizen Information Service of Illinois. *Steps in Writing A Proposal.* Chicago: CISI, 1976.

Dermer, Joseph. *How to Write Successful Foundation Presentations.*
A manual on proposal writing. Includes approaches to use for hard to fund programs; largely for social action programs.

Evaluation Handbook. San Francisco: Public Management Institute. (n.d.)

Ezell, Susan (Ed.). *The Proposal Writer's Swipe File.* Washington, DC: Taft Corporation. (n.d.)
Includes fifteen professionally written proposals that can servie as models for writing and design.

Hall, Mary. *Developing Skills in Proposal Writing.* Portland, OR: Continuing Education Publications, 1981.

Particularly geared to proposals dealing with training, demonstration, and service programs rather than research activities. Special emphasis on forms involved in government funding.

Jacquette, F. Lee, & Jacquette, Barbara I. "What makes a good proposal." *Foundation News,* January 1973.

Kiritz, Norton J. *Program Planning and Proposal Writing.* Los Angeles: Grantsmanship Center, Reprint Series, 1980.

A classic piece, used as the basis of all Grantsmanship Center training workshops.

Krathwohl, David R. *How to Prepare A Successful Research Proposal.* Syracuse, NY: Syracuse University Bookstore.

Lefferts, Robert. *Getting a Grant: How to Write Successful Grant Proposals.* Englewood Cliffs, New Jersey: Prentice-Hall, 1982.

Strong on the basics; easy-to-follow step-by-step procedures.

Needs Assessment Handbook. San Francisco: Public Management Institute. (n.d.)

Orlich, Donald C., & Orlich, Patricia R. *The Art of Successful R&D Proposals.* Pleasantville, NY: Redgrave Publishing, 1977.

Smith, Craig. *Getting Grants.* New York: Harper & Row, 1980.

A creative guide to the grants system: How to find funders, write convincing proposals, and make your grants work.

The Grant Writer's Handbook. San Francisco: Public Management Institute, Volume I (1978) and Volume II (1980).

Each volume is loaded with how-to tips, outlines, checklists.

White, Virginia. *Grants: How to Find Out About Them and What to Do Next.* New York: Plenum Press, 1975.

Chapter 9

DRAWING UP THE BUDGET

When I got to the budget part of my proposal, I thought I was over the hump. Was I ever wrong! By the time I had costed out what we intended to do, it totaled $256,000. The funder's average grant for last year was under $80,000. Not much chance that we could get what we needed for the project.

And there was just no way we could trim what we were planning to do without so emasculating the program as to make it relatively worthless. I should have started with the budget, then figured out what we could do with the limitations imposed. We would probably have designed a different project, or looked for alternative sources, maybe even more than one source of support.

The program planner quoted learned the lesson too late. There was no longer sufficient time to go back to the drawing board and redesign prior to the funder's application deadline. You can do better, but it will take some understanding of the budget-making process.

The budget is both a program and a fiscal document. Think of it as a plan expressed in financial terms. It details how much you intend to spend (in dollars) for what (personnel and materials, activities, or end results) over a designated period of time. Because the budget permits you to put what you propose to do and spend down on paper, it provides you with an instrument to monitor your activities in both

---

Author's Note: Much of this chapter is adapted from Chapter 12 of Armand Lauffer with Celeste Sturdevant, *Doing Continuing Education and Staff Development.* New York: McGraw-Hill, 1978. A more detailed discussion of the budgeting process is found in Chapter 11 of Armand Lauffer, *Strategic Marketing* (tentative title). New York: Free Press, forthcoming.

programmatic and fiscal terms. Budgets are generally presented in tabular form, the budget table being explained in a narrative "budget justification."

THREE KINDS OF BUDGETS

There are different kinds of budgets. Each has its own advantages and disadvantages. The *line budget* is probably the one most administrators are familiar with. It is the most commonly used. Budget lines list expenses just the way they are paid out. Typically, line items for continuing education programs include personnel, consultants and instructors, facilities, equipment, consumable supplies, and travel.

The *performance budget* projects the cost of performing a certain unit of work, for example, conducting a workshop, counseling clients, managing a project. It reflects the work to be done and anticipates the cost of doing any given number of units of work. A properly designed performance budget might even show the relative savings of increasing the number of units of work. For example, because overhead expanses remain fairly stable, it may cost $160,000 to retrain forty unemployed workers, and only half that much to train forty more. The cost may get progressively lower until it levels off at about $1500 each trainee when the project contracts to train 150 or more.

A *program budget* goes one step further. It categorizes expenditures in relationship to the agency objectives or the objectives of a particular project. Administrative and maintenance costs are allocated to specific objectives, such as placing retrained workers on the job, getting a hard-to-place child adopted, or completing a plan for staff and organizational development, or producing instructional materials. The examples in Table 9.1 may help you visualize the differences among these budgets.

You'll notice that the line-item budget tells you exactly what you expect to spend money on. For that reason, it makes it easy to monitor your expenditures. It is a good device for tracking the outflow of funds, but it has several disadvantages, First, by focusing on the expenditure of resources rather than on accomplishment, it does little to reflect the purpose of those expenditures. The budget is considered merely an accounting device. It is not very helpful in designing your program. The program or project, in fact, has to be fully designed before its objectives or activities are translated into budgetary terms. Because line-item budgets don't say enough about *why* each item is included, they generally require explanations that appear in a budget narrative following the budget summary. These explanations or justifications are sometimes given in performance or program terms.

The performance budget describes the work authorized or projected. It aggregates the items found in the line budget. Thus the category of

Table 9.1 Simplified Line-Item, Performance, and Program Budgets Compared

Line-Item Budget		Performance Budget		Program Budget	
Personnel	$20,000	Consultation		Plan	
Consultants	6,000	on program design and		for staff	
Facilities	2,000	development		develop-	
Equipment	1,000	of plan	$6,500	ment	$11,500
Supplies	2,000	Staffing of		Instruc-	
Travel	1,000	planning committee	3,000	tional materials	20,500
		Design of instructional			
		materials	18,000		
		Printing	1,500		
		Administra-			
		tion	3,000		
Total	$32,000		$32,000		$32,000

consultation and program design in the performance budget includes personnel, consultants, supplies, and travel expenditures from the line-item budget. The program budget, focusing on outputs, aggregates further. In the comparison chart the two products are a plan and instructional materials. Expenditures under each include those categories found in both the line-item and the performance budgets. For example, the plan will require consultation on program design, staffing of planning committees, and some of the funds allocated to general administration found in the performance budget. It can also be broken down into line items.

THE LINE-ITEM BUDGET:
A CLOSER LOOK

Because line-item budgets are most common, it might be helpful to describe what goes into each item and then make a number of suggestions about what to consider in assigning a dollar value to each line item.

Personnel. Includes estimates of the salaries (including raises) and fringe benefits that will be paid to all personnel employed by the agency or project. Fringe benefits and employee pay are generally posted separately as two items on the budget document, but may be combined as a single item. Personnel includes full- and part-time staff who perform professional, clerical, maintenance, and other supportive tasks. Indicate on your budget if personnel are to be full or part time. One way of doing this is to specify the full time equivalent (FTE). For example, five FTE would indicate that salaries sought cover the equivalent of five full-time employees in a particular category. In point of fact, these might be for ten half-time employees. Five FTE would indicate a single person working half time or several persons sharing the equivalent of a half-time person. In your narrative you may have to justify the number or categories of personnel and explain your use of several people to equal one FTE.

Consultation and Contract Service. This includes services required by the project that its staff are unable to provide. Consultation services are performed by individual consultants or organizations with whom you contract. Anticipated fees as well as expenses incurred by consultants in providing service (for example, travel and per diem) may be posted as a single item on the budget document or be broken down into several cost estimates. Your narrative can be used to justify costs.

Facilities. Includes space required by the project to administer and perform its activities. Space may be leased, rented, purchased, or donated as an in-kind contribution. If space requires remodeling or renovation, these costs should also be distinguished as a line item on the budget document and the rationale for altering the site should be outlined in the budget justification. Remember that few funders are likely to cover renovation or purchase costs for projects that are not expected to last beyond one or two years.

Equipment. Includes both office and program equipment such as furnishings, typewriters, and audiovisual (AV) equipment that staff use in administering or carrying out activities. Costs appearing in the category of equipment may represent items purchased or rented. An explanation of the need for special or costly pieces of equipment should appear in the budget justification. Note that it may be possible to lease equipment that the agency can purchase for $1 or some minimal sum on completion of the project.

Consumable Supplies. Includes office supplies such as typing materials and stationery, lavatory supplies, and other commonly used and less expensive office implements, such as staplers and in-baskets. It also includes paper, film, books, and other supplies used in your service programs. Communication and telephone costs may also be included, although if they are expected to be high, they may require a separate category. Include estimates of the costs of monthly rental, or charges for long-distance telephone calls, and fees that might be charged for radio, television, and newspaper announcements. Printing and reproduction costs may be included here or may go into a special program or publications category. Cost estimates might include the rental of equipment required to print or copy materials as well as the costs of purchasing reproduction machinery or having the work performed by an outside contractor.

Travel and Per Diem. This item includes estimates of the travel expenses that will be incurred by staff and volunteers within the local area, when leaving the local area to carry out agency business, and, occasionally, travel expenses incurred by consumers participating in agency activities. Per diem costs include expenses for room and board incurred when staff or clientele must leave the local area to participate in activities or perform business meaningful to the operation of the program. Expenses for consultant travel and per diem may be included in either the consultant or the travel category of the budget document.

You'll find that most funders — your host organization, a foundation supporting a project, another agency contracting for your services, or a federal bureau with a grants program — have their own instructions for designing a line-item budget. Be sure to follow their instructions or guidelines. If you've never put a line-item budget together, you might find the format on the sample budget in Table 9.2 helpful.

DESIGNING THE LINE-ITEM BUDGET

Line-item budgets are generally divided into two major categories: personal and nonpersonal items. The "tabular" budget is usually followed by the "budget justification." Budgets should be designed to communicate all necessary details to relevant audiences. If you are using a funder's guidelines, make sure that you follow those guidelines to the letter. If you are following the procedures generally used in your own organization, make sure you understand those procedures and that you use the categories considered standard for other programs and departments.

Table 9.2 Sample Line-Item Budget for a Training and Materials Development Project*

Line	Requested	Donated	Total
1. Personnel			
a. Professional (percentage of appointments/length of appointment)			
(1) Director at $24,000 (.125 FTE)**		$3,000	$3,000
(2) Associate Director for Materials Development at $20,000 (.25 FTE)	$5,000		$5,000
(3) Trainer/Evaluator at $18,000 (.5 FTE)	$9,000		$9,000
b. Nonprofessional			
(1) Secretary at $10,000 (.25 FTE)		2,500	2,500
(2) Bookkeeper at $20,000 (.05 FTE)		1,000	1,000
(3) Maintenance people at $10,000 (.05 FTE)		500	500
c. Fringe benefits (22% of above)	3,080	1,540	4,620
2. Consultants			
a. Six consultants @ $200/day for 5 days each	6,000		
b. Travel and per diem (one trip per consultant)	3,000		9,000
3. Nonpersonnel			
a. Equipment			
(1) 50% purchase price of typewriter and desk	1,000		
(2) Rental of audiovisual equipment as needed	500		1,500
b. Consumable supplies			
(1) Office consumables (paper, typewriter ribbons, etc).		600	
(2) Telephone (monthly charges plus long-distance costs)		400	
(3) Consumable instructional materials		1,200	2,200
c. Staff travel			
(1) Mileage at reimbursable rate of 24 cents per mile for 2000 miles		480	
(2) Four out-of-town trips @ $200 each		800	1,280

Table 9.2 Continued

Line	Requested	Donated	Total
d. Facilities			
(1) Rental of office space	1,200		
(2) Rental of conference			
facilities		800	2,000
TOTAL***	$28,780	$12,820	$41,600

   *   This budget does not include indirect costs. Most host organizations charge indirect costs on the basis of either total direct costs (TDC) or a percentage of the personnel costs.

  **   In the budget justication, this is described as 25% time for six months.

***   In this budget, the applicant is contributing almost 45% of the amount needed for the project in both out-of-pocket and in-kind donations. Which are the in-kind donations?

Referring to the Table 9.2, let's look at the anatomy of a fairly standard line-item presentation. Notice that there are three columns: one for the *total* budget, one for the *requested* amount, and another for the *denoted* amount.

The *total* budget projects what the program will actually cost, regardless of sources of income. The "requested" column specifies the amount you are requesting from a particular source, say the United Foundation, the Community Mental Health Board, the City Council, the Federal Office of Human Development, the local Kiwanis organization, or Litton Industries. The "donated" column refers to all other sources.

For different audiences you may wish to use different categories. Instead of the "requested" and "donated" categories, for example, you might prefer designations such as *sponsor*, or *cost sharing*. If you have several sponsors, you might wish to divide the *"requested"* column further for each of the sponsors to whom you are submitting a proposal. If other suppliers have already committed funds, include a "committed" column. In this case the *"donated"* column would reflect only your own organization's contributions. Should you be seeking funds primarily from the organization's *general fund* or other internal source, the columns might include "general fund allocation," "fees from clients," and "parents appeal campaign." Clearly, there are many possibilities. Budgets are flexible tools. Design yours to communicate what is significant in your circumstances. The categories you decide to use should be determined by what you hope to convey to the publics you are addressing.

The tabular budget must include as much information as possible, but no more than is needed. This may become clear when we examine each of the line items. Let us begin with Personnel. The section on personnel generally includes three subsections: (1) salaries and wages,

(2) fringe benefits, and (3) consultants and contract services. You might wish to further subdivide salaries and wages into "professional personnel" and "support staff."

Indicating the specific salary allocated to a given staff member may be insufficient without designating the number of months that person will be working on the project or the percentage of work time allocated to that project. Assume that the project director's annual salary is $24,000, but he or she is assigned only quarter time to the project. Assume further that you are asking the funding source to cover the full 25 percent of his or her time allocated to the project for the entire twelve months. Here is how you could communicate this as a line item.

	Requested	Donated
Project Director: .25 FTE at $24,000	$6000	—

Suppose your project includes five caseworkers. The next line item might then read as follows:

	Requested	Donated
Caseworkers: 5 FTE at $20,000	$80,000	$20,000

In this case the agency or some other donor is contributing 20 percent of the salaries from some other source. If one of those workers is already on staff, this might be the agency's *in-kind* contribution. You may wish to explain this in the budget justification. If you expect to be refunded the next year, that explanation may be crucial. Some budget writers prefer to designate each item that is to be subsequently explained with an asterisk (*) or some other symbol; others prefer to use superscript numbers much as they might footnote in a professional article; still others prefer none of these designations, trusting that the reader will understand what is being communicated when reading the justification section.

If you expect salaries to change due to union contracts or annual merit increments during a given or fiscal year, you will want to show this in the budget as well. Do so by designating that the project director will be paid for three months at $24,000, and nine months at $26,000. If you decide not to use FTEs this is how you might show it on your line-item budget:

	Requested	Donated
Project Director at 25 percent of $24,000 for 3 months and 25 percent of $26,000 for 9 months	$6250	—

In FTEs this would still amount to .25. It might be written as 0.25 FTE $[(24,000 \div 4) + 3(26,000 \div 4)]$. A similar procedure would be used for each of your professional and support staff: the secretaries, clerical assistance, bus drivers, maintenance personnel, accountants, and others.

Let us assume you have decided what work needs to be done, and how many people it will take to do the job. Each job is given a title. So far so good; the trouble is, you are not sure how much each person should be paid. What to do? The first step is to find out what comparable programs, within your organization and outside, pay staff who have similar responsibilities. Is there a going rate in your agency and in your community for certain jobs? Pay rates on newly funded projects should neither exceed nor fall below pay rates for comparable positions elsewhere in your agency. This same holds true for pay raises and fringe benefits.

If some or all of the staff to be assigned to the project are new, you will have to make some guesses about where, on a range of possible salaries, each might be placed. Assume for a moment that the salary for a caseworker ranges from $18,000 at entry level to $28,000 per year for those at the upper end of the scale. If you estimate too low, say close to the $18,000 beginning level, you will not be able to attract more experienced or expert staff persons. If you start too high, your funders are likely to be suspicious fearing that you are padding the budget. As a rule of thumb, it is helpful to divide the salary range into six segments. In this case, it would be $18,000, $20,000, $22,000, $24,000, and $26,000, the upper limit being $28,000. You would not want to hire all the staff at the upper level with no hope of advancement. Pick the anticipated salary level for the new employees somewhere at the middle or just above the middle range, say $22,000 or $23,000. This is the figure you will use in your line-item budget. In the sample line-item budget we assumed a narrower range of $18,000 to $22,000 for the associate director, with a midpoint upon which the request was made of $20,000.

FRINGE BENEFITS

Fringe benefits are generally calculated as a percentage of all salaries and wages. If you work for an established organization, chances are that these average about 22 percent to 26 percent of total salaries and wages for all professional and support staff. However, there may be separate fringe packages for different categories of staff, with differential agency contributions to health, life insurance, or retirement benefits for various categories of staff. All will include mandatory workmen's compensation and FICA (social security), which accounts for 10% or more of salaries and wages.

The fringe package may also include voluntary contributions to (1) health, mental health, and dental health insurance programs; (2) an annuity or retirement fund; (3) life insurance; or (4) to some other benefit program. Some organizations also provide what has come to be known as "perks." These may include payment to attend training programs, memberships in professional associations, access to agency services and facilities, subsidized rent, use of an agency vehicle, and so on.

If your organization has already developed a fringe package, use the percentage allocation in your budget; otherwise you will have to design a new one and justify it.

CONSULTANT AND CONTRACT SERVICES

Remember: These are services your staff does not have the competence to perform and which it is cheaper to contract for. Be especially careful to detail consultant and contract costs. Funders are likely to be suspicious if the fees you pay are high. Here again, you will have to check on the going rate. Recognizing that some consultants demand much higher fees than others, your agency may have to establish an upper limit beyond which it will not go in paying consultants. The reason why consultants are not listed as professional staff under the "salary and wages" category is that they do not receive fringe benefits.

NONPERSONNEL ITEMS

Look over the sample line-item budget. Most items are self-explanatory. Remember that unusual items or costs must be explained in the budget justification. Let me take up a few that might cause you some grief if they are not properly addressed.

Whatever is requested for travel must be reflected in the program narrative. If part of that program includes a transportation service for the elderly or for other clients, in contrast with the travel costs anticipated for staff, you would not include those costs on this line.

Develop a separate line item called "transportation service" in the "program expenditure" column. That line might even include several sublines dealing with maintenance and repair, parking and garaging, and so on.

Trainee travel costs and appropriate per diem expenses may be allowed. Check this item and any restrictions. No sense in having a whole project rejected because you were unaware of the funder's limits.

Out-of-town travel for staff is probably one of the most vulnerable sections of the budget. If you have a regional or statewide project, and that project requires that your staff travel to sites throughout the area, that travel will generally be considered local in nature because it deals with your program's locality. Out-of-town travel refers only to the trips outside of the locality in which the organization provides its services. The reasons for such travel might include participating in professional conferences, meeting with staff of comparable or sister projects in other parts of the country, attending staff training programs, and so on.

The designation "other costs" can be used as a catchall for a variety of items like: (1) fire, theft, and liability insurance; (2) dues to professional organizations; and items that do not seem to fit anywhere else. If, however, they are of central importance to the project, they should have their own category. Suppose you intend to design a series of how-to guides or video tapes for use in community education. This probably should have its own line with a number of subitems such as typesetting, printing, binding, addressing, and mailing.

INDIRECT COSTS

Now let's talk a little bit about one of the least understood aspects of the budgeting process: the request for indirect costs. Although the direct costs (those we have been discussing so far), may be easy to identify, they may not be so easy to specify. For example, if the project in question is located in an existing agency, new office space and equipment may not be necessary. Accordingly, there is no need to request line-item funds for space leasing, utilities, maintenance, and the like. These are costs typically incurred for common purposes in the operation of the total organization. The project does, however, use agency office space and equipment and the maintenance that goes with them. Such items can be legitimately charged to the project, but the exact costs involved may be difficult to ascertain. To reflect these real costs, you may be permitted to charge a percentage of all salaries and wages or of the total expenses as indirect costs. In this case you would not also list them elsewhere as line items.

Check with the funder about what is allowable. Do not overlook indirect costs. Without them a project can end up costing the agency a great deal. Note that in many cases, a funder will not pay indirect costs but will permit the agency to use these as a required match. In this case, they would go in the *"donated"* column.

COST-SHARING

When used this way, indirect costs become part of the applicant organization's *cost-sharing* effort. Many government and foundation awards require some form of cost sharing or *local match*. Any real cost to a project, whether direct or indirect, may be counted in cost sharing. Examples include fees paid by consumers, staff effort devoted to a project at no cost to the sponsor, and services (such as maintenance). In some cases the time contributed to a project by volunteers can be used for cost-sharing purposes. However, this is a bit tricky. You will have to check with your sponsor to find out if this is, in fact, permissible. When volunteer time is used, you will have to spell out the actual dollar value of the time contributed before you can locate it in your "donated" column. There are generally two accepted ways of doing this. The first is to find out what the going rate would be for a comparable service if purchased in the open market. The second is to determine what the volunteer would be earning if employed for money elsewhere.

Other contributions may include consumer fees; third-party payments (for example, insurance company payments); the income from a fund raising campaign or endowment; or funds contributed by another funding source — a local foundation, business corporation, civic association, or the United Way.

It is not enough to claim costs are shared. Anything in the "donated" column is as subject to audit, as are requested funds. You may be asked to document staff and volunteer time actually allocated to the project.

BUDGETS ARE STATEMENTS OF INTENT; INTENTS CHANGE

Budgets are plans written in tabular form. As with other plans, they are subject to review and modification if original projections prove to be unfeasible. Most funders will permit you to make minor adaptations in the budget without demanding prior approval. Permission is rarely required to make adaptations of 10 percent, more or less, on any given line item, or any line item category (such as professional personnel). Thus, if the project director's salary winds up to be lower than you anticipated, but a caseworker's salary turns out to be somewhat higher, and all this does not exceed the 10 percent limit, it will not be necessary for you to ask permission prior to hiring the person in question. A 3 or

4 percent reduction in personnel expenses, if those funds are shifted to consumable supplies, may result in the 25 or 30 percent raise in the amount of money allocated toward supplies. You will need permission from the sponsor before making that change.

GETTING AUDITED

The nice thing about "donated" and "requested" columns is that it shows the funder what the money requested is to be spent on. This is what will be examined should your project be audited during or subsequent to its completion. To prepare for an audit, you will have to do an accurate job of accounting. Accounting refers to those ongoing activities involved in maintaining an updated and accurate record of the flow of income and expenses related to a project. Accounting is used to ascertain that income and expenses are in line with projections in the budget. The idea behind accounting is to make sure that money is not only spent as prescribed, but also at a rate of expected or available income. Unless the rates of expenditure and of income are in balance, or in favor of income rather than expenditure, the program may find itself in considerable trouble.

Audits refer to periodic examinations of the fiscal records involved to see whether or not income and expenditures go according to plan (the budget). The auditor considers whether or not the amounts expended on specified items were proper, whether the sources from which money was drawn were proper, whether the timing was appropriate, and whether documentation of each of these was correct. Audits may be conducted internally or externally.

Internal audits are generally conducted by an accountant or other staff member within the organization itself. External audits may be conducted by the sponsor or funder or by an outside agent acting on behalf of the sponsor. Audits are sometimes conducted two or three years after a project has concluded its activities. Thus, it is not only important to maintain good records, but to keep them for a minimum of three to five years.

WHAT FUNDERS LOOK FOR IN BUDGET REQUESTS AND SUBSEQUENT AUDITS

Funders are going to scrutinize your budgets carefully. Exercise 9.1 is followed by a checklist of issues they are likely to concentrate on. Use them to go over your own budget prior to submitting it to agency administration or to a potential funding source.

EXERCISE 9.1
DESIGNING YOUR OWN BUDGET

Now it is time for you to try your hand at budget design.

(1) Pick a program or project that requires a new or revised budget. It might be the program you began planning as you worked on the exercise in the previous chapter, a current agency program that is expected to expand or to be cut back next year, a fund-raising drive (these also require financial outlays and require their own budgets).

(2) Design a tabular line-item budget. Make certain that all anticipated expenses are included. Decide which are to be requested, and which are to be donated. If your organization has a salary scale, travel reimbursement policies, a regular fringe benefit package, and so on, use the figures and percentages recommended by the agency's fiscal manager. If it does not, find our what other organizations in your community do, or what the funder will permit. As your guide, use the outline in Table 9-2, a budget previously submitted by your organization for this or another program, or the budget format suggested by the funder. If you intend to use your budget to submit to a funding agency be certain that the funder's instructions are followed.

(3) Write up the budget justification of the line-item tabular budget, explaining any items that might be questioned or that may seem out of line, or that are not clear from the program narrative you may have written for the exercise in Chapter 8. Justify your projected expenditures in program and/or performance terms.

(4) Now translate the line-item budget into either a program budget, a performance budget, or, for additional experience, do both. For example, should you be designing a budget for a fund-raising campaign, the performance budget might aggregate expenses under the following categories: brochures, letter campaign to general audience, dinners and banquets, solicitor recruitment and training, administrative costs, and so on. The program budget might focus on the achievement of campaign goals, and these might be divided into such categories as pacesetters, medium-sized givers, general public. For each you would have a target goal in terms of funds raised, and a breakdown or expenses needed to raise those funds. How might you break down the Sample Line-Item Budget in Table 9.2 into program and performance terms? Look for clues in Table 9.1.

(5) On completion of your budget table and narrative, review it the way a funder might. Use the Funder's Checklist.

FUNDER'S CHECKLIST

(1) All budget items are justified in the text of the proposal, the narrative, and in the budget justification. No important items have been left out of the budget.

(2) Each figure is properly explained unless it is clearly self-explanatory.

(3) The budget designates *requested* and *donated* sums or uses some other designation to convey what is required of the funder and of the recipient.

(4) The budget is broken down into logical segments: personnel, nonpersonnel items, indirect costs, and so forth.

(5) Budget figures are realistic. For example, fringe benefits are not out of line, salaries are compatible with local standards. The costs are reasonable and made in relationship to concerns for efficiency.

(6) Out of the ordinary costs (high telephone or travel costs) are fully explained in the budget justification.

(7) The total size of the budget is appropriate to the project itself.

(8) Line items represent not only reasonable estimates of current cost, but include estimates of future costs, taking into account inflation or changes in salary rates.

(9) The proposal is tailored to the funder, and follows the guidelines or procedures and forms required by the funder.

(10) Figures total properly. The writers know their arithmetic.

SUMMARY

The budget is a program and fiscal document. It can be used to plan programs and services, anticipate cash income and outflow, and hold the organization accountable for what it sets out to do. It is not an immutable document, however, and should be changed in relation to changed circumstances or modified program objectives.

The most common budget categorizes all of its expenditures into line items. These items are generally divided into two major sections: personnel and nonpersonnel. Personnel items may include salaries and wages for professional and other personnel, the fringe benefits they receive, and fees for service from consultants and outside contractors. Other nonpersonnel items include rental, leasing, and related expenses; disposable office supplies; program supplies; and equipment. A number of programs or projects may also include travel and per diem expenses for staff, board members, trainees, and so on.

All line-items must be consistent with the program narrative in a project plan or proposal (as when a project application is submitted to an outside funding source). Items may need to be further explained in a "budget justification" section that generally follows the "tabular" budget. This justification is generally couched in program or performance terms. Performance budgets describe the cost of performing certain program activities and generally relate to the functions or work of distinct operational units. They are most useful in describing the work planned or authorized and are useful management devices. Program budgets focus more directly on the purposes of an operation and the goals and objectives to be reached.

The accounting process is aimed at tracking funds in to and out of an organization or program, and checking on whether the rate of income is adequate to cover the rate of expenditures. The auditing process is used periodically to determine whether the expenditures are proper and according to plan.

SUGGESTIONS FOR FURTHER READING

Fortunately, there is a growing literature on budget development and design. If there is a budget officer in your organization, it may not be necessary for you to design the budget on your own. In many cases the funding organization will provide you with all the guidelines you need in order to design the budget according to acceptable standards. If you wish to read further, however, the following two items should prove most helpful.

Vinter, Robert, & Kish, Rea, *Budgeting and Fiscal Management for Nonprofits* (tent.). New York: Free Press, forthcoming.
This is a thorough account of the budgeting process; no better document is available to nonprofit organizations.

Lohman, Roger. *Breaking Even: Financial Management in Human Service Organizations.* Philadelphia: Temple University Press, 1980.
Goes beyond budgeting to examine ways of accounting for and pricing services to reduce the likelihood of deficits.

In addition, the national association that your organization may be directly or indirectly affiliated with should also have materials available for you. The following are excellent examples.

Budget Presentation: Some Guides for Family Service Agencies. New York: Family Service Association of America, 1969.
Budgeting: A Guide for United Ways and Not-For-Profit Human Service Organizations. Rosslyn, VA: United Way of America, 1975.

Other useful documents include:

Budgeting for Nonprofits. San Francisco: Public Management Institute, (n.d.)
Carter, Reginald. *The Accountable Agency: Everybody Cares But Nobody Knows.* Beverly Hills, CA.: Sage, 1983.
Gross, Melvin J., & Warshauer, W., Jr. *Financial and Accounting Guide for Non-Profit Organizations.* New York: Ronald Press (John Wiley), 1974.
Hall, Mary. *Developing Skills in Proposal Writing.* Corvalis, Continuing Education Publishers, 1981. See Chapter 12.

Jones, Reginald, & Trentin, George, *Budgeting: Key to Planning and Control.* Washington, DC: American Management Association, 1971.
Lauffer, Armand. *Strategic Marketing* (tent.). New York: Free Press, (forthcoming).
Standards of Accounting and Financial Reporting for Voluntary Health and Welfare Organization. New York: National Health Council, 1975.

Chapter 10

WHAT TO DO IF YOU DON'T GET FUNDED
And What to Do If You Do or
While You're Waiting to Find Out

VIGNETTE 15:
TWO VIEWS OF REVIEWS

WHAT TO LOOK OUT FOR
(View Number 1)

Things went according to clockwork. The NIMH panel did a preliminary review of our proposal. We passed the first hurdle. Dr. Milton, one of the project officers, called and arranged to make a site visit with one of the members of the external review panel. A visit was scheduled for mid-April. I had five weeks to arrange our end.

I called representatives of the other agencies with whom we would have to collaborate if we got funded, sent them copies of the proposal, and invited them to one of the sessions during the site visit. One of NIMH's evaluative criteria was the extent to which there was involvement and commitment by other service providers.

The site visit went beautifully (although one of the secretaries was a little nervous and went overboard in preparing coffee and cake); beautiful until we got to the afternoon meeting with the other agency people.

One of them was very supportive, although she had obviously not thought through all of the ramifications for her agency. Sondra Kravel of the Child Guidance Clinic sat through the first half of the session reading the proposal; then she started asking questions, even suggesting changes in the proposal. Well, that opened things up. Dr. Sussman tried to cue her in. These were not issues to discuss before the site visitors. But the cat was out of the bag, and some of the other agency representatives joined in, each trying to improve the proposal.

You guessed it. We did not get funded. The reasons: agency collaborators had not adequately been involved in project design and improvements were still possible. We could, if we wished, resubmit during the next funding cycle. Problem was, we would have to wait six months, and the staff we wanted to assign to the new project would not be able to wait that long to find out if they had jobs or not. What a bummer!

WHAT TO LOOK FOR
(View Number 2)

Given a choice, I would award a grant to the person whose proposal is loosely written, but who I know from experience will do a thorough and honest job. I would be less likely to award a grant to a person whose proposal is beautifully and concretely written, but whose reputation for producing leaves something to be desired. Still, there are other considerations. It's not easy to be a reviewer.

Sometimes even the best-written proposal from the most reputable source gets turned down. I've sometimes recommended funding for projects coming from what I consider to be lousy agencies. The reason is simple. They're in a neighborhood that needs service, and they won't be able to offer the service without the project and the funds it will bring. If it means pouring good money into a second-rate agency that's going to provide at least some useful services to a minority community, that gets almost nothing from anybody, I'll vote to put the money over there. I see it as being part of my responsibility as a public official to contribute to the redistribution and relocation of resources where they are needed the most.

Now that's my bias, and I'm honest about it. But I'm professional enough to know that I can't act on that bias alone. Making effective decisions on proposals requires being clear about the overall priorities of your own agency. Even though we've got a set of regulations that spells out many of these priorities, each proposal forces us to reexamine our values.

Our regulations, for example, include clear statements about the "right to service" and the "universality" of those services. The "regs" make it clear that social services should be available to all people as a matter of right, and that eligibility for a service is to be based on need relative to the purpose and function of that service, without regard to a person's ability to pay. The plan also makes it clear that services should be accessible to everybody at whatever point they may choose to enter.

But we've got another statement in our "regs" that says that the resources should be allocated where they're needed most. It specifically identifies low-income neighborhoods and ethnic minorities that do not currently have easy access or entry into the service system. When a proposal comes in that talks about establishing a multipurpose center for Cuban refugees, we've got a hard decision to make. The proposal clearly meets the criterion for putting resources where the need is greatest, but are we negating our principle of universal right to service? No people other than Cuban refugees would be using the center.

We have a couple of other policy statements, too. One is that social services should permit consumer choice and should allow for the protection of individuality and consumer participation in policy making. Now those are nice principles, but they're not always operable. If a good proposal comes in that doesn't include consumer participation in policy making, but does protect the consumers by providing them with a variety of grievance mechanisms, we're likely to fund it. Another project might come in that doesn't allow for grievance machinery and in fact threatens the principle of confidentiality simply because clients are involved in policy making. How do we choose?

Reviewers do not always find it easy to make the right choice. If the criteria for the review process create dilemmas for panelists, how can the proposal writer be sure that the right issues have been stressed and the right form used? There are no hard and fast rules. But there are some things you can do to increase the likelihood of success.

In this chapter we will examine how proposals are reviewed and by whom. Careful attention to a number of critical issues will increase your organization's likelihood of getting funded. But the processes involved in grantsmanship are not completed when you have satisfied yourself that the proposal is the best you are capable of. There are things to do even after the proposal has been posted in the mail. We will, therefore, also consider what you should do while you are waiting to get the results of the grant or contract review process, what to do if you do not get funded, and what to do if you do. Finally, we will discuss what you can do if your grantseeking efforts yield results beyond your expectations. But first, we will examine the criteria by which proposals are reviewed, and what happens to the proposal after you send it off.

GETTING REVIEWED

All grantseekers should know something about how proposals are reviewed and by whom. If the information is not available in the proposal kit or other information you receive from the funder, you may have to do some investigating. The best way to find out is by asking the funding source itself.

Federal agencies generally use external panelists to review research, training, or service-oriented proposals. Panelists who are considered to be expert in their fields are often brought to Washington for one day to a week to review proposals that have first been screened by staffers for appropriateness (Was it submitted to the right agency?) or for correctness of form. Be aware that if the proposal arrives after the deadline for submission, is prepared on the wrong form, or is incomplete, it will not generally pass the initial screening. Panelists will be given a *proposal rating sheet* for the proposals that pass. Typically, the sheet will instruct reviewers to score each proposal on a five-point scale on the basis of the following criteria:

- *Significance* — that is, importance of objectives, generalizability of impact;

- *Procedures or Program Description* — completeness, precision and detail, compatibility with stated objectives, knowledge of related work, overall design or organization, realistic timetable, and so on;

- *Personnel and Facilities* — qualifications, organizational structure, availability of nonfiscal resources;

- *Economic Efficiency* — how expected results relate to relative costs.

- *Feasibility* — can the work be done as described?

Proposals that score the highest are put in one pile, those that are clear rejects go into another, and those in between go into a central pile.

If all panelists agree a proposal should be funded, there is a strong likelihood (assuming funding levels are adequate), that it will be approved. If everyone agrees that other proposals should not be funded, they will not be. The panelists may be convened as a group to examine the middle pile, or to discuss their reasons for differences of opinions on the others. For example, if five panelists feel a proposal should be funded, but two are not sure and one feels that it should not, a resolution will be arrived at through discussion intended to yield consensus.

Recent efforts to cut the cost of government spending have led federal agencies to eliminate Washington-based reviews. Panelists may be asked to rate proposals at home. Discrepancies in judgment may also be resolved through correspondence or through telephone conference calls. The site visit described in the vignette with which I opened this chapter is becoming a thing of the past except in the more costly or high priority federal programs. In some cases, particularly when sole-source contracts are at issue, or when the funds to be allocated are discretionary, the review may be made by a single federal official or by a panel of officials.

State-level funding decisions are much more variable. The procedures may change from year to year or from agency to agency. Some use external panels but most rely on staff decisions within the agency making the grants or contract awards. Often state and federal departmental decisions are subject to review by the office of the budget or the governor's budget priorities committee, which may determine that an expenditure being projected is incompatible with overall government spending priorities. The budget office can hold up, and sometimes reject a proposal that has otherwise overcome all other hurdles.

Local government grants rarely go through an external review panel. Line staff in appropriate departments (e.g., recreation, housing) may be entrusted to issue contracts or grants. On some programs—for example, community development block grants—a citizen's review board or council may be established by the mayor or the city council to review and approve all grants and contracts. The staff may be asked to recommend action, but the discussion belongs to the board or council. This process sometimes gets extremely political.

Foundations generally rely on staff to make decisions. On small grants such decisions may be made by individual foundation staffers or department heads. Larger grants may be reviewed by the foundation's board of trustees, or by a special review panel that deals with a particular sector of the foundation's work. But the board or panel members involved will rely to a large extent on staff recommendations. This, of course, refers to the larger foundations. When it comes to the smaller family foundations, decisions may be made by the person who gave it its initial endowment, by a member of the family, or by a trustee entrusted with such responsibility. The trustee, perhaps an attorney or a banker, may know little of the subject matter or of your agency, and so may rely on someone else in the community for advice.

Corporation grants are generally made by executive officers. If the corporation is not accustomed to making grants and has not established a procedure for making them, the review may be made by the executive officers or a community relations officer entrusted with the responsibility. Since the process of involving the private sector in human service issues is still highly idiosyncratic to the organizations and communities involved, it is too early to be able to describe prototypic patterns. You may have to help design those patterns in the community where you work.

In contrast, the United Way and other well-established fund-raising and allocating bodies in the voluntary sector tend to have highly formalized review processes. Those were described in Chapter 6. Staff members work closely with applicant organizations, and guide lay committees organized into sector review panels in the decision-making process. Most of these decisions are focused on whether to increase or decrease allocations based on the previous year's experience. New applicants may be put through a particularly rough review process that examines not only the application itself, but also the problem or population to which it is addressed, and the capacity of the organization making the application to do the job specified.

For civic associations the populations to be served may be the most important concern. Association members may not feel they have the capacities to make judgments about the applicant organization or how it has chosen to serve those in need. The decision may be made by an executive committee or a community services task group, but will generally have to be ratified by the board or the entire membership at an open meeting.

Understanding these differences may suggest alternative actions on your part both before and after the proposal has been submitted. We will discuss these shortly. First, I want to share with you some insights on why proposals are sometimes rejected. We will focus primarily on the federal government because it continues to be the major source of funding for the human services and because its procedures are the most standardized and well understood.

WHY PROPOSALS ARE REJECTED

Several years ago, in a review of some 605 disapproved research grant applications, the Public Health Service determined that rejections were made on the basis of the following shortcomings: the problem (58 percent), the approach (73 percent), the investigator (55 percent), and other reasons (16 percent). Note that these are not necessarily real weaknesses, only a reflection of a poorly expressed or sketchy proposal. Let us dig a bit further.

Of those proposals rejected because of the problem being investigated, more than half were determined to be of insufficient importance or as being unlikely to produce any useful information. Of those rejected because of the approach used, half were determined to include scientific procedures that were unsuited to the stated objective, more than a third described the approach to be used in so nebulous a manner as to preclude serious examination, and about one out of six were judged to have a poorly thought-through study design.

Investigators (project directors) were rated low especially when they appeared to have inadequate experience or training to conduct the particular research in question, because the investigator appeared to be unfamiliar with recent pertinent literature and methods, or because his or her published work in the field did not inspire confidence. Other issues related to unrealistic requests for equipment or personnel, unfavorable institutional settings, and the assumption that the project director would devote insufficient time to the project.

These reasons for rejecting research proposals are not that dissimilar from reasons given for turning down training- and service-related grant applications.

Have you heard of other reasons for rejection? Make a checklist of possible issues to look out for according to your own experiences or to the types of proposal your organization is preparing, perhaps to the funding source it will be submitting those proposals. Use the checklist for evaluating proposals being developed by colleagues and acquaintances. You may learn as much from evaluating others' efforts as you did in writing your own proposal. You may learn even more from getting others' feedback and incorporating it in a redesign effort.

Before we move on, I want to focus on two issues touched on by the persons quoted at the start of the chapter. As the applicant to NIMH learned, it is sometimes not enough to say all the right things in the proposal itself. It may be as important, or more, to get other people to corroborate your claims. A well-designed proposal was rejected because the other key players did not understand the rules of the game; they fought over the ball when they should have been passing it to each other.

The funder quoted in the second vignette spoke of the importance of fitting a proposal to the purpose of the missions of the funding agency. This is a point I have been making throughout the book. I want to reiterate it. No one is going to fund your organization because it thinks it is doing the Lord's work. Your support will come from others who are convinced that you are doing *their* work, and in the best manner possible.

WHAT TO DO WHILE YOU'RE WAITING

What should you do while you are waiting to find out if your application has been approved? Keep busy! There may be lots more work to be done.

(1) Update the proposal if necessary.
(2) Promote the proposal or the ideas behind it among relevant publics.
(3) Design a fall-back plan in case you do not get funded.
(4) Gear up for operations in case you should get funded.

We will take these one at a time.

It is not unusual, under the press of deadlines, for proposal writers to submit a less than perfect document. There are also times when circumstances change, and a modification in the narrative or the budget may be necessary. Funders will generally permit you to modify a proposal if you submit a letter with necessary supporting documents. This is almost always true if your materials get there before the review process takes place. For example, the results of a United Way survey may come in two weeks after you have submitted the proposal to a federal agency. If those data support your argument, summarize them and send them in with a note asking that the summary be added to the appendix. If financial support is to be forthcoming from a source mentioned as a possibility in the proposal (e.g., gift from a foundation, or from a wealthy philanthropist), inform the potential grantor to whom the application was made, and modify your budget request

accordingly. If new letters of endorsement or support arrive after you
have mailed the proposal, send them in and ask that they be added to
your file.

Promotional activities during the period of review or just before it
can pay significant dividends. Not long ago, I submitted a grant
application to a federal agency. The Michigan Department of Social
Services was anxious that the University of Michigan get the grant.
State officials informally, through telephone calls and on visits to
Washington, made it clear that the project was in the state's interest.
Members of the congressional staff of one of the Michigan representatives, who was himself on some pretty powerful committees, also let the
word out that Michigan was interested in the project. A word of
caution here: informal influence, especially when well orchestrated, can
be very effective; but it can also backfire when it is perceived as pressure
or as an organized campaign.

This may be less true at the local level, particularly when citizen
support is active and vocal, and when a case is made in noncontrover-
sial terms. Local officials and citizens' task groups are going to listen to
organized voters who know what they want and are willing to articulate
their demands in ways that are not going to be insulting or that will not
cause opposition or backlash from other quarters. When a proposal is
submitted that deals with an issue that is poorly understood, press
coverage of the issue (not necessarily about the proposed intervention
program) is likely to help educate and sensitize decision makers in a
way that even the best-phrased program design cannot.

A proposal submitted to the United Way or to a local corporation is
likely to be received positively if officials in the corporation or lay
leaders in the United Way are knowledgeable about your agency and
the issues it intends to tackle. Their opinions may carry more weight
than those of others. It may not be appropriate for you to approach
them directly. It may be much more helpful if a board member from
your agency or another friendly advocate does the communicating with
the decision makers in question.

WHAT TO DO
IF YOU DON'T GET FUNDED

What should you do if you do not get funded? The answer will be
clear if you are prepared with a fall-back position. The nature of that
position should depend on the centrality of the proposal to your
organization's operations. If it is very central, if the organization cannot
do without the grant, your fall-back position should include alternative
sources of funding. There is rarely any rule against support from more
than a single source. Funders may ask you whether a similar proposal

for support has been submitted elsewhere. You will need to so inform them. And if you do get support from several sources, you will not be able to pocket the difference or to use if for something you have not been funded for. You may have to inform the funder that you are willing to accept a smaller grant because you have gotten partial support elsewhere, or request a modification of the proposal that may expand the program or modify it to include the additional resources.

If the project is rejected, are there some ways in which you can hang on by reducing services, by using volunteers, by delaying start-up? Always find out why the proposal was rejected. If the funder does not deal with the kinds of issues you proposed, find out if there is a more appropriate source of supply. If the proposal itself is wanting, find out how it might be improved, whether you can submit again, and when.

WHAT TO DO IF YOU DO GET FUNDED

What should you do if you do get funded? You will know if you spent the time between submission and approval in gearing up. More than once I have heard from a funder, as late as August or September, that a program was approved that is to start up on October 1. Once, the word came down in mid-October (after the projected starting date), for a project that had to be completed by the end of the fiscal year—the following September 30. To avoid wasting start-up time, start seeking staff and getting needed facilities or equipment before you get final word. You may not be able to hire staff before you have the grant award, but you can start the interviewing process early; and you can negotiate with appropriate persons in your organization for the reallocation of staff from other responsibilities. You will need to make an informed judgment about the likelihood of getting funded. No sense in investing too much effort in a long shot. However, there is not much sense in being caught high and dry because of lack of preparation.

What if you get funding for an amount smaller than you requested? Your fall-back plan should take this possibility into account as well. The allocation may be too small to conduct even a modified program. Other sources of funds may not be available. In this case, you may have to reject the grant. Alternatively, it may be possible to delay start-up time or to modify the objectives and the activities and yet achieve some of the goals you set forth. It may also be possible to reallocate funds from some other agency operations.

Sometimes it pays to do less than we might wish, for no reason other than to establish a relationship with a funder. This is a professional decision and it may not be an easy one to make. Remember that "a difference that makes no difference, is no difference." It may not be worth the effort for the agency, the staff involved, or those the original project design was intended to help. There may already be too much going on in your organization that is of little or no benefit to anyone. Why compound the difficulties by taking on something that no one really needs?

Let us assume you do get the award, you have started the program or project, and things are looking well. Great. But it is still not time to rest or sit on your laurels. There may, in fact, never be a time to sit back. Just as programs need constant attention, so do funding sources. Funders will want a careful accounting of what you are accomplishing and how close you are to your original design and to your timetable. They will want to know how the funds are being spent. Quarterly, semiannual and final reports may be necessary. Put as much time and effort into these as you did in your original proposal. You may know that you are doing well, but the funder will need to know this too.

Get the reports into those places where they will do most good. The local press is one place. Papers delivered at professional conferences or published in journals are other places. Send the funders copies of those articles and reports as they appear. Include testimonials from those who have been effectively served or who can honestly report on the significance of the project. Make certain that these are phrased so as to articulate with the funder's concerns and priorities.

Remember that a grant is rarely a lifetime commitment. What happens when the grant period is over? What could happen if a three-year grant is not funded after the second year because of a government cutback or a change in funding priorities? You will need a contingency plan that guarantees continuation. Who should be involved in the design of that plan? Who else cares?

Perhaps it is appropriate that I end this book with a question. That, after all, is the way we started. I will resist the temptation, however. Instead, I will leave you with a thought. Successful agencies generally do pretty well at raising funds and getting grants. Organizations that have been successful in raising funds and getting grants, are considered to do pretty well at other things. That may seem redundant. It is not. Samuel Butler phrased it in a more ingenious way.

"A hen," he said, "is an egg's way of making another egg."

Appendix A

GETTING THE TERMS STRAIGHT

COMMON AND TECHNICAL TERMS ASSOCIATED WITH GRANTSMANSHIP AND FUND RAISING

Accounting: the classifying, summarizing, and recording of financial and related transactions.

Agreements: exchanges between two or more groups or organizations for a variety of commodities and actions. Purchase of Service agreements are essentially contracts for specific services that the contracting agency is mandated to perform but which it finds more effective or efficient to contract out.

Allocation: act of assigning resources to an organization or subunit.

Annual Appropriation: regular allocation of funds for ongoing budget or program, generally from the same source to the same recipient; sometimes modified to reflect inflation, program growth, or program cutback.

Application Kit: information provided by the potential funder about what is desired, the procedures that must be followed, and often including abstracts or summaries of grants given out in previous years.

Appropriation: budget making by a legislature or other public body.

Audit: periodic investigation of financial statements and their relationships to planned or permitted expenditures.

Award: the sum of money given by a contracting or granting agency to cover all or part of the sponsored project's costs.

Budget: a plan for anticipated expenditures, activities, and accomplishments stated primarily in fiscal terms.

Types of budgets:

(1) *Line-item* — budget format organized in tabular and narrative form, in which expenditures are listed as items, each on their own lines, that describe expenditures.

177

(2) *Performance* — budget format in which costs of performing sets of interrelated activities are aggregated.

(3) *Program* — budget format in which costs are related to outcomes and expectations.

Campaign: organized activity aimed at inducing others to behave in specifically determined manner; as in fund-raising campaign.

Cash Flow: actual movement of money in and out of an organization or subunit; negative cash flow signifies that outflow is greater than income; whereas positive cash flow signifies that income exceeds expenditures.

Constituency: aggregate of individuals and/or organizations that support or can be mobilized for support of an individual or organization, and to which he or she/it/they are in turn responsible.

Contract: an award given for a specific activity in which the funder has specified all the terms (e.g., who can apply, exactly what is to be done, and how, at what cost, and by whom).

Types of Contracts:

(1) *Sole-Source* — where only one party is asked to apply because of the source's specific and unique qualification.

(2) *Open-Bid*: competitive situation where anyone meeting the general qualifications for a particular type of contract can bid for it; RFPs are generally posted and information on them distributed broadly.

(3) *Fixed Price*: contract in which the size of the award is fixed at start. No cost overruns may be allowed.

(4) *Cost Reimbursement*: contract in which the grantee's costs are fully reimbursed; a maximal limit may be set, but this is subject to review in relation to changes in prices, problems in technology, and so on.

(5) *Cost-Sharing*: agreement in which two or more organizations (one of which may be the recipient) share in the cost of the project.

Donors: persons who make cash or material contributions to the organization and its programs.

Fees: money payments made for a service by consumers or a third-party payer such as an insurance company.

Funders: organizations that give grants and award contracts.

Fund Raising: a process of identifying and soliciting potential donors and grantors, and of obtaining money through campaigns, sales, or grantseeking.

Grant: a type of award that is supportive in character, given for a specific purpose, yet permitting the recipient considerable latitude in determining what is to be done, for whom, when, how much, and within limits, at what cost.

Types of Grants:

(1) *Block Grants* — the mechanism by which grants are made to a unit of government (state, regional, or local) for such broad purposes as housing or employment, as authorized by legislation or administrative policy. Recipients have great flexibility in distribution of those funds and may

themselves become grantors or funders within the broad purposes of the grant according to the criteria established by the original grantor.

(2) *Categorical Grants* — funds that are expended for specific purposes, generally by the recipient unless used by the recipient for the purchase of a service that can be provided better or cheaper by a third party.

(3) *Formula Grants* — determination of size of awards to be provided to specified grantees on the basis of a specific formula prescribed in legislation or regulation rather than on the basis of individual project review. Formulas may be set on basis of such factors as population, per capita income, age, and so on. For example, the Administration on Aging may use a formula that includes the proportion of the elderly in the population, the number of those people who fall below the poverty line, the square mileage of the area, and the extent to which it is urban or rural in determining how much money is available to each state, or to subregions within states.

(4) *Discretionary Funds* — awards in which the funding agency or its chief officer has considerable latitude in deciding who can receive funds and for what amount, so long as it falls within the general policies or guidelines governing the funding source.

Grantee: the individual, group, or organization that is the recipient of a contract or grant award.

Grantor or Contractor: the individual or organization making a specific award.

Grantseeking: a process of identifying, soliciting, and proposing activities aimed at getting grant or contract awards.

Guidelines: general information on how to complete a proposal and specification of the issues that must be addressed in a grant application (proposal). Frequently these are found in the application kit. Guidelines must be meticulously followed; improperly submitted or written proposals, especially those that go to government and foundation sources, are likely to be disregarded.

Income: flow of money and in-kind resources to an organization or subunit.

Indirect Costs: a budget item that refers to the costs incurred by the grantee that are difficult or impractical to itemize but that can legitimately be charged to the program.

Marketing: aggregate of activities aimed at the exchange of commodities and services between suppliers, producers and consumers. The marketing of social services includes reaching out to and involving many publics in the exchange of resources and services.

Opportunity Costs: values forfeited by investing time and other resources in certain activities, precluding the possibility of making like investment in other activities.

Price: the cost attached to a service or activity, usually in financial terms, but also in psychological and social terms.

Private Foundations: organizations that have charitable, religious, educational, scientific, or cultural purposes. When identified as philanthropic foundations, they are primarily in the business of funding causes, programs, organizations, and individuals they consider worthwhile.

Types of Foundations:

(1) *Independent* — foundations have their own board of directors and are not affiliated with any other government or private sector organization, or responsible for doing any organization's business other than their own.

(2) *Community Foundations* — often receive some operating funds from local government, and are concerned primarily with local cultural, human service, and economic development needs.

(3) *Family Foundations* — are generally established for charitable or religious purposes and managed by members of the family that endowed the foundation, or their trustees.

(4) *Company Foundations* — are the creatures of business enterprises and are often established to funnel the company's charitable contributions into area that benefit the company, its employees, or the communities in which the company is located.

(5) *Operating Foundations* — solicit funds for their own purposes, allocate them to their own activities, and do not generally fund outside organizations or groups.

Program: a set of interrelated activities aimed at the production of a service or some other outcome.

Project: a program which is time bound and has a relatively clear set of objectives.

Project Officer: official in government or foundation responsible for a particular grant or contract program.

Promotion: activities aimed at advancing an idea, a cause, a program, or an organization; increasing consumer or public receptivity to a product or service; consciousness raising.

Proposal: a plan of action (always in writing when applying for a grant or contract) describing what is to be done, for what purpose, how, by whom, when, and at what cost.

Types of Proposals:

(1) *Solicited Proposal* — one that is requested by a potential funding source (grantor or contractor) that has originated the ideas for the program or project, often through an RFP.

(2) *Unsolicited Proposal* — one in which the idea for the project clearly originated with the proposal writer or submitting agency (potential recipient).

Public: aggregate of persons or organizations that have characteristics in common, or that are perceived by an organization as having a specific and functional relationship to it.

Types of Publics:

(1) *In-put Publics* — provide the organization with the legitimacy of the resources it needs in order to conduct its business.

(2) *Throughput Publics* — turn resources into programs and outputs.

(3) *Output Publics* — are the consumers or recipients of products and services.

Resources: all the means and commodities needed to produce and distribute a product, or achieve an objective.

Revenue: cash income.

RFP: Request For Proposals, generally communicated in writing and sometimes posted in public documents such as the *Commerce Business Daily* or the local press. The term "RFP" was once used exclusively to refer to requests for contract proposals, but it is now increasingly used to refer to grants as well.

Site Visit: visit made by one or more representatives of the grantor to the grantseeking organization in order to get details on applicant's capacity to do work proposed.

Sponsored Project: a specific complex of activities or program financed by funds other than those of the regular budget of the group or organization (sometimes the individual) administering the project. For example, if your agency regularly provides services to the disabled through allocations from the United Fund, but receives a special additional subvention from the United Fund to establish a home-based program, or receives a grant from a government agency to do so, this is considered to be a "sponsored project" because funds outside of the normal allocations of the organization are used for the project and the sponsor (funder) can be readily identified.

Appendix B

GRANTSMANSHIP INFORMATION RESOURCES

Look over the suggested information resources in this Appendix, but do not be limited by it. You will find a much wider array of suggestions in the narratives and suggested readings for Chapters 2 through 9. What follows are a number of additional resources that I thought you might find useful. They are divided into four sections: (1) magazines and periodicals, (2) training organizations, (3) search services, and (4) multipurpose fund-raising books and guides.

MAGAZINES AND PERIODICALS

Federal Grants and Contracts Weekly

You already know about the *Commerce Business Daily* and the *Federal Register* (see Chapter 3). The *Weekly* uses those sources to select information nonprofit organizations find useful. It contains information on the latest RFPs (requests for proposals), grants, and contracting opportunities, newly issued federal regulations, and closing dates for grant programs.

It can be ordered from Capitol Publications, 1300 North 17th Street, Arlington, Virginia 22209.

Funding Review

A quarterly review of government, private sector, and foundation funding sources, it features articles on management, book reviews, and selected grant deadlines. Order it from the National Grant Development Institute, 1135 North Garfield, Pocatello, Idaho 83204.

Grants Magazine

Many of its articles focus on the technical aspects of researching government, voluntary, and private sector sources. The magazine, which tends to be of equal interest to funders and grantseekers alike, can be ordered from Plenum Press, 233 Spring Street, New York, New York 10013. It is a quarterly.

Independent Sector

Articles, resource opportunities for both health and welfare are included. A new publication, it focuses on needs of the voluntary and private sectors, but includes descriptions and critiques of government programs. It is available from the Independent Sector, 1828 L Street, NW, Washington, D.C. 20036.

LRC Newsbriefs

Resource materials on program development and government grant programs are made available on a monthly basis from the Lutheran Resources Commission, 1346 Connecticut Avenue, N.W., Washington, D.C. 20036.

The Grantsmanship Center News

A bimonthly publication written in everyday and down-to-earth language, the News is printed in an attractive, easily accessible format. It contains articles on planning and program design, grantseeking and proposal writing, budgeting and fiscal management, fund raising and resource development. It also publishes information on categorical grant programs and deadlines, new directions in foundation grantmaking and other materials of interest.

Currently, between fifty and sixty reprints are available with such titles as:

Anatomy of a Grants Process — Federal Funding for Health
Basic Guide to Salary Management
Contractsmanship
Cost Accounting for Non-Accountants
Exploring Corporate Giving
Funding for Women's Programs
Grantsmanship Resources for Rehabilitation Programs
Guide to Public Relations for Nonprofits
How to Develop a Fund Raising Strategy
How to Use the Catalogue of Federal Domestic Assistance
IRS and Charities
Marketing Nonprofits
Obtaining Funding from Local Government
Researching Foundations
Special Events Fund Raising
The Oil Companies as a Funding Source

For information on subscriptions and a full list of reprints, write to the Grantsmanship Center, 1031 South Grand Avenue, Los Angeles, California 90015.

TRAINING AND TECHNICAL ASSISTANCE ORGANIZATIONS

The Grantsmanship Center (see information on *Grantsmanship Center News*) is a nonprofit organization that conducts five-day workshops in locations throughout the country. At present, three types of workshops are sponsored: Proposal Writing and Program Planning, Fund-Raising Training, and Program Management. Workshop sessions are designed to include mini-lectures, well-designed resource kits, and ample opportunity to engage in a design process with consultation from trainers.

Subscribers to the journals described above, or to search services listed below will receive periodic information on other training opportunities offered under university, foundation, or publisher's auspices. Check also the conferences and continuing education programs of the professional associations to which you belong.

The following organizations also provide some technical asstance and occasional training workshops. Write to those that interest you and find out what services they provide.

Alcoholics Anonymous
P.O. Box 459
Grand Central Station
New York, NY 10017

Alternative Medical Association
7915 S.E. Stark Street
Portland, OR 97215

American Association of Fund-Raising Councils
500 Fifth Ave.
New York, NY 10036

American Council
for the Arts
570 7th Ave.
New York, NY 10018

American Hospital Association
800 North Lake Shore Drive
Chicago, IL 60611

American Nurses Association, Inc.
2420 Pershing Rd.
Kansas City, MO 64108

Association of Volunteer Bureaus
P.O. Box 125
801 North Fairfax Street
Alexandria, VA 22314

Center for Community Economic Development
1320 19th Street, NW
Washington, DC 20036

Child Study Association of America
67 Irving Place
New York, NY 10003

Community Education Skills
Exchange Network (CESEN)
c/o Program for Community
Education Development,
AOB IV
University of California
Davis, CA 95616

Council for Financial Aid to
Education
680 Fifth Ave.
New York, NY 10022

Council of Jewish Federations
575 Lexington Ave.
New York, NY 10022

Family Service Association of
America
44 East 23rd Street
New York, NY 10010

Federation of Protestant
Welfare Agencies
281 Park Ave. South
New York, NY 10010

Gray Panthers
3635 Chestnut Street
Philadelphia, PA 19104

Institute for Responsive
Education
704 Commonwealth Ave.
Boston, MA 02215

Institute for Voluntary
Organizations
175 Jackson Blvd.
Chicago, IL 60604

International City Managers
Association
11200 G Street, NW
Washington, DC 20005

Mental Health Association
1800 N. Kent Street
Rosslyn, VA 22209

National Association of
Accountants for the Public
Interest
45 John Street
New York, NY 10038

National Association of
Community Health Centers,
Inc. (NACHC)
1625 I Street, NW, Suite 420
Washington, DC 20006

National Association for
Retarded Citizens, Inc.
2709 Avenue East
Arlington, TX 76011

National Association of Retired
Persons
1909 K Street, NW
Washington, DC 20049

National Catholic Development
Conference
119 North Park Ave.
Rockville Center, NY 11570

National Center for
Community Action
1328 New York Ave., NW
Washington, DC 20005

National Center for Prevention
and Treatment of Child
Abuse and Neglect
1205 Oneida Street
Denver, CO 80220

National Center for Urban
Ethnic Affairs
Institute for Nonprofit
Management Training
1244 Maryland Ave., NE
Washington, DC 20001

National Center for Voluntary Action
1214 16th Street, NW
Washington, DC 20036

National Council on the Aging
1828 L Street, NW
Washington, DC 20036

National Health Council
20 W. 40th Street
New York, NY 10018

National League of Cities
1301 Pennsylvania Ave., NW
Washington, DC 20004

National Rural Center
1828 L Street, NW, Suite 1000
Washington, DC 20036

National Training and
Information Center
1123 W. Washington Blvd.
Chicago, IL. 60607

National Urban Coalition
1201 Connecticut Ave., NW
Washington, DC 20036

Public Interest Public
Relations, Inc.,
225 West 34th Street
New York, NY 10001

The Alliance for Justice
600 New Jersey Ave., NW
Washington, DC 20001

The Center for Community
Change
1000 Wisconsin Ave., NW
Washington, DC 20001

The Support Center
1709 New Hampshire Ave., NW
Washington, DC 20001

The Volunteer Urban
Consulting Group
24 West 40th Street
New York, NY 10018

United Way of America
810 North Fairfax Street
Alexandria, VA 22314

Women's Action Alliance
370 Lexington Ave.
New York, NY 10017

Women's Funding Assistance
Project
Ms Foundation
370 Lexington Ave.
New York, NY 10017

SEARCH AND DETAILED INFORMATION SERVICES

There are a number of search services available that will provide you with information on funding sources that may be tailored to your needs. These can be rather expensive. You might want to consider sharing a subscription with another organization. Do not ignore the additional information sources of the Foundation Center described in Chapter 4.

Aris Funding Messenger

Every six weeks Aris publishes a *Creative Arts and Humanities Report*, and a *Social and Natural Sciences* (including health) *Report*. The latter also includes updates between reports. For more information, write to Aris, 2330 Clay Street, San Francisco, California 94115.

Funding Sources Clearinghouse

A matchmaking service for fund raisers and grantors, FSC sends out a monthly news digest, occasional bulletins, and practical guides on proposal writing. It offers unlimited access to computerized search services and telephone consultation. The service is nonprofit, but not cheap, unless you calculate it in hours saved. Its data bank has over 50,000 corporate, foundation, and government entries. Brochures and costs are available from the Funding Sources Clearinghouse, 2600 Bancroft Way, Berkeley, California 94704.

ORYX Press Grant Information System

Subscribers receive a loose-leaf reference volume, one each year, that includes grant programs listed by deadline and subject matter or interest, grant name, and sponsoring organization. It covers a wide variety of government (federal, state and local), foundation, corporate, and association sources. Quarterly updates and monthly bulletins are issued in six categories: health, humanities, creative and performing arts, life sciences, social sciences, and education. For more information, write to The ORYX Press, 7632 East Edgemont Avenue, Scottsdale, Arizona 85257.

The Taft Information System

The oldest foundation information subscription system, Taft publishes several annual publications including the *Foundation Reporter*, *The Corporate Foundation Directory*, *Trustees of Wealth*, and the *News Monitor of Philanthropy*. The *News* is a monthly publication that includes articles on philanthropy and recent grants, events, or noteworthy gifts. A *News Service Hotline* keeps subscribers up-to-date on funding opportunities in specified areas of interest. For information write to Taft Products, Inc., 100 Vermont Avenue, NW, Washington, D.C. 20005.

Publicly supported search services include the following:

ERIC (Educational Resources Information Center)
National Institute of Education
U.S. Department of Education
Washington, DC 20208

HSIC (Human Service Information Center)
1408 N. Fillmore Street, Suite 7
Arlington, VA 22201

National Center for Education Statistics
Statistical Information Office
Presidential Building, Room 205
400 Maryland Ave., SW
Washington, DC 20202

National Clearinghouse for Alcoholic Information
P.O. Box 2345
Rockville, MD 20852

National Clearinghouse for Drug Abuse Information
P.O. Box 416
Kensington, MD 20795

National Clearinghouse for Mental Health Information
Public Inquiries Section
5600 Fishers Lane
Rockville, MD 20857

NTIS (National Technical Information Service)
U.S. Department of Commerce
5285 Port Royal Road
Springfield, VA 22161

FUND-RAISING BOOKS AND GUIDES

The items below tend to cut across government, foundation, and private sector sources and for that reason may not have appeared in the suggested reading section of Chapters 3 through 6.

Funding in Aging. Garden City, NY: Adelphi Press, 1979.

Grantsmanship Money and How to Get It. Chicago: Marquis Academic Media, 1978.

Health Grants and Contracts Weekly. Capitol Publications, Inc., Suite G-12, 2430 Pennsylvania Avenue, NW, Washington, DC 20037.

Heywood, Ann M. *The Resources Directory for Funding and Managing Nonprofit Organizations.* New York: Edna McConnel Clark Foundation, 1982.

President's Task Force on Private Sector Initiatives, *Project Bank.* President's Task Force, 734 Jackson Place, NW, Washington, DC 20400, 1983.

Private Funding for Rural Programs. Washington, DC: National Rural Center, 1978.

Sweeny, Tim, & Seltzer, Michael, *Fund Raising Strategies for Grass Roots Organizations.* Washington, DC: Community Careers Resource Center, 1982.

Tax Economics of Charitable Giving. Chicago: Arthur Anderson 1982. (revised periodically)

ABOUT THE AUTHOR

Armand Lauffer, editor of the Sage Human Services Guides, is one of the most prolific authors in social work. His Sage volumes include *Getting the Resources You Need, Assessment Tools for Practitioners, Managers and Trainers* (both of which have been selected by the National Association of Social Workers for distribution to its membership), *Understanding Your Social Agency* (with Lawrence Zeff), *Volunteers* (with Sara Gorodezky), among others. Recent textbooks include: *Social Planners at the Community Level, Doing Continuing Education and Staff Development, and Strategic Marketing.* Two new books on personnel practice and human resources management will shortly be published by Sage.

Dr. Lauffer is Professor of Social Work at the University of Michigan. He has written grant applications for, and managed, more than twenty projects funded through federal, state, foundation, private sector, and international sources. He lectures and consults frequently on grantsmanship and resource development in the United States, and is a consultant to a number of Israeli universities and government welfare agencies.